REVOLTING

www.penguin.co.uk

Also by Terry Deary

A History of Britain in Ten Enemies

REVOLTING

A RIOTOUS HISTORY OF REBELLIONS AND REVOLUTIONS

TERRY DEARY

bantam

TRANSWORLD PUBLISHERS

UK | USA | Canada | Ireland | Australia
India | New Zealand | South Africa

Transworld is part of the Penguin Random House group of companies
whose addresses can be found at global.penguinrandomhouse.com.

Penguin Random House UK, One Embassy Gardens,
8 Viaduct Gardens, London SW11 7BW

penguin.co.uk

Penguin
Random House
UK

First published in Great Britain in 2025 by Bantam
an imprint of Transworld Publishers

001

Text design by Couper Street Type Co.

Typeset in 12.5/17pt Adobe Jenson Pro by Six Red Marbles UK, Thetford, Norfolk
Printed and bound in India by Manipal Technologies Limited

The authorized representative in the EEA is Penguin Random House Ireland,
Morrison Chambers, 32 Nassau Street, Dublin D02 YH68.

A CIP catalogue record for this book is available from the British Library.

ISBNs:
9780857507600 (cased)
9780857508645 (tpb)

Penguin Random House is committed to a sustainable future
for our business, our readers and our planet. This book is made
from Forest Stewardship Council® certified paper.

MIX
Paper | Supporting
responsible forestry
FSC
www.fsc.org   FSC® C018179

This book is dedicated to the true heroes of history,
Mr and Mrs Peasant

'Disobedience, in the eyes of anyone who has read history, is man's original virtue. It is through disobedience that progress has been made, through disobedience and through rebellion.'

OSCAR WILDE, 'THE SOUL OF MAN UNDER SOCIALISM', 1891

CONTENTS

INTRODUCTION

THE REVOLTING ARE ALWAYS WITH US

How revolting are you? It's something you ought to ask yourself. You may swear you are the least revolting person you know but are you really? Don't you take the side of the rebel? Don't you cheer for Robin Hood rather than the Sheriff of Nottingham? Don't you quietly suppress a sigh when revolting peasant Wat Tyler is stabbed by the weedy Richard II's henchman? Or wipe away a tear for Joan of Arc as her dreams of freedom go up in smoke (along with her body)?

We need to understand our fellow humans, but first we need to understand ourselves. One of the many measures of your personality is where you stand on rebellion: are you a conformist or ready to take arms against a sea of troubles?* If you think you are a conformist, are you sure there's nothing that would make your rebel spirit spring out from under the duvet?

You have plenty of material out there. The history of the world is a history of rebellion, from Day One up until today and probably long into the future.

Ashurbanipal, the last great king of the Assyrian Empire, was

---

* Good phrase. Note to self: use it in a playscript some time.

not a man to be trifled with. In 667 BC he invaded Egypt to finish off what his dead granddad Sennacherib had started.

Sennacherib (ruled 705–681 BC) had promised those who resisted his rule . . .

I cut my enemy's throats like lambs. I cut off their precious lives like string. Like the waters of a storm, I make the juices of their throats and guts run down onto the wide earth. My prancing horses plunge into the streams of their blood as they would into a river. The bodies of their warriors filled the plain. I tore out their private parts like the seeds of cucumbers.

You may be fined for refusing to pay your television licence but at least you get to keep your private parts. (Probably.) When it was Ashurbanipal's turn to repress Egypt, many of the Egyptian nobility were executed and the Assyrians ruled for twenty painful years. Like his granddad – it must run in the family – Ashurbanipal was a cruel ruler who had his promise carved onto a monument . . .

I had the arms and legs cut off their bodies and I fed them to the dogs, pigs, wolves and eagles. I fed them to the birds in the heavens and the fish in the oceans. What was left I had taken from Babylon and thrown into heaps. I broke into the tombs of the old Elamite kings and let in the sun. I carried their bones back to Assyria. I stopped the priests giving them sacrifices so their ghosts were tormented.

As deterrents against insubordination go, that is stronger than detention at HMP.

It seems rebellion is just part of our nature. In the Bible, God tells Adam and Eve they may eat any of the fruit in the Garden of Eden but not the apple. So, what did they do? You know it. An evil serpent persuades them to have a nibble. As a punishment, we humans were thrown out of Eden and left to hunt and gather for ourselves. 'That'll teach them to rebel,' God said. She already had her own problems with Lucifer – a rebel angel. God's answer to Lucifer's disobedience was to order him to get the hell out of heaven. Not God's smartest move: the exiled can still plot and organize a comeback. Still, defying authority has consequences. Rebel if you want, but face punishment if you fail (especially if you live in ancient Assyria).

If you're not persuaded by lessons from the Bible, then look at the Greek cautionary tales. Prometheus rather liked the primitive little humans. Zeus told Prometheus not to give the pathetic primates the gift of fire. Prometheus disobeyed, which is just as well otherwise a lot of us would still be shivering while eating raw mammoth. Unfortunately for Prometheus, Zeus chained him to a rock on Mount Caucasus. Every day, an eagle would claw its way into his side to nosh on his liver (no onions). That liver would regenerate overnight, and the torment would start all over again. Prometheus suffered this torture for centuries until, eventually, Hercules freed him by slaughtering the eagle and breaking the fire-thief's chains.

You may notice another salutary lesson in there. The poor old eagle was only doing its job. Those people who, through history, have carried out the punishments – the hangmen and the jailers, the assassins and the law enforcers – are on the front line when rebels strike back. When the Peasants' Revolt kicked off in

1381, the cry was, 'Kill the lawyers!' But it was Sergeant-at-Arms John Legge at the Tower of London who stood in the way of the rebels and was butchered. He wasn't a lawyer trying to enforce the unpopular Poll Tax. Legge wasn't even a solicitor. He was just in the way.

The Peasants' Revolt happened because King Richard II had needed the Poll Tax to fight the Hundred Years' War over in France and expand his power. Richard II was not killed. Sergeant-at-Arms Legge was. Had the war gone ahead, Richard would have employed some of those revolting peasants as infantry to fight and die for his ambitions. The peasants were being asked to pay a tax for the privilege of risking their lives in a battle that didn't benefit them. Meanwhile Richard would have stayed safe by the fireside at home (thanks, Prometheus). You can understand why the peasants were miffed and resorted to cutting off the heads of the powerful and fastening them on poles.*

Many people through history have claimed that violence is never the answer. Really clever people like Mahatma Gandhi (1869–1948) who said, 'Victory attained by violence is tantamount to a defeat, for it is momentary.' Momentary or not, three bullets fired into the chest of Gandhi by Nathuram Godse put a permanent end to the pacifist.

It's tempting to ask what Gandhi's views would have been on the events of 20 July 1944, when Claus von Stauffenberg led the plot to assassinate Adolf Hitler. He took a briefcase packed with

---

* Presumably they secured the heads using pole tacks.

explosives into a meeting with the Führer. The bomb was placed next to Hitler, but an aide called Heinz Brandt moved it unknowingly to one side. When it exploded, one of the table legs shielded its target from the blast and the Charlie Chaplin lookalike escaped with scorched trousers. (Brandt was killed and it's hard to resist saying, 'Serves you right'.) Almost five thousand people were arrested and executed in revenge. The Second World War would be over the next year, but in that year an estimated 60 to 80 million people lost their lives, including a staggering 55 million civilians. All those millions died because a single act of violent rebellion failed.

Not many events in the history of revolt are on as dramatic a scale as that plot. Most people will say the assassination attempt on Hitler was the right thing to do. A huge majority of Americans would argue that the assassination of Abraham Lincoln is at the 'wrong' end of the spectrum. (There will always be a lunatic fringe who argue that Lincoln's assassination was 'right', but we can ignore them because they are lunatics.) The problem is that very few rebellions are as clear cut as those examples, and they probably won't be when you make your own choices in the future, even if you are armed only with a pencil in the ballot box.

How far would you go to fight an injustice? Simply put, there are three stages:

Riot: a public act of violence by an unruly mob, which sometimes leads to . . .

Rebellion: open opposition to authority. Rebellions are usually unsuccessful. Because if they succeed they become a . . .

Revolution: the overthrow of rulers by the ruled.

When rebels win the language shifts. 'Rebels' become 'freedom fighters'. As Napoleon said, 'When the mob gains the day, it ceases to be the mob. It is the nation.'

What would turn your grumbling into open rebellion? What would persuade you to stop grumbling and act? If failure meant you faced ruin, torture, death or disembowelment, is there anything that would motivate you to act against the status quo? What revolting situation could strike a rebellious chord in you?

The world is waiting on your answer.

REASON TO REVOLT 1
MONEY

'Poverty is the parent of revolution and crime.'
ARISTOTLE (384–322 BC) – GREEK PHILOSOPHER

People rebel because they hope that if they win they will be better off. And that has sometimes meant better off financially. In the words of the sainted Tom Cruise in the movie *Jerry Maguire*, our rebels may scream, 'Show me the money.'

Taxes have always been a source of discontent. It's not the principle – you pay a share of what you have, and the community gets a benefit. No, it's the inequity of forking out when those richer than you don't, or it's the way your taxes are spent. You love the roads your taxes went to pay for but the un-mended potholes drive you to distraction . . . or rather they stop you driving to distraction – or anywhere else – because your cart has broken a wheel.

Then there are those who want something they think is rightfully theirs, but have it purloined by the powerful. A revolt will reclaim your inheritance. If it doesn't get you killed of course.

MARCUS LICINIUS CRASSUS, 115–53 BC

Crassus ruled the empire alongside Julius Caesar. He set up schools for slaves and educated them to a high standard. What a humanitarian, you cry? No. He had an ulterior motive. He ensured his trained slaves were given jobs with the most influential Romans. There they could spy on their new owners and report their secrets to Crassus. Those secrets made him rich and also helped keep him safe from his enemies. He became known as the richest man in Rome thanks to a career primed by his daddy's millions. (Any resemblance to a US president is simply coincidence.) He used his wealth to buy his way into power and succeeded.

He had been exiled in Spain from 87–84 BC but used his money to finance a private army of 2,500 men. They in turn multiplied his investment by bullying and plundering cities in the region. He then joined with the rebel Sulla to march on Rome and take over. A successful revolution had begun. The trick was to hang on to that power. Money would be needed to bribe, appease and mollify opposition. The great thing about being in power is you can generate money. Crassus set about amassing a fortune in a way that Scrooge would have approved of if he had been invented 1,900 years earlier.

Sulla punished his enemies by confiscating their property and selling it off cheaply. First in the queue with his toga full of sesterces was Crassus. His property dealings, along with a lot of slave trading, meant his wealth grew to around 200 million sesterces. (In modern money, that is a lot.)

For those who wish to become multi-millionaires, here is a

tip. Find a burnt-out house and buy it cheap from the desperate (uninsured) owner. Rebuild it even cheaper – using the enslaved labourers that you own – and end up owning a large part of Rome.

You may like to imitate Crassus's even more evil trick, if you are so inclined: set up your own fire brigade. Rush to the scene of a fire but refuse to put it out until the owner agrees to sell for a knock-down (or burnt-down) price. After your bargain-basement brickies have rebuilt it you may generously let the poor owner rent it back. Hod luck, mate.

Crassus's rise looked unstoppable. Not even a scandal of criminal intimacy with a woman could stop him. (Any resemblance etc.) The woman in question was a vestal virgin, and purity was in her job description. Any man found guilty of violating her sacred condition would be publicly beaten to death. Crassus was sent for trial. His defence? Crassus said, 'I was not interested in her body, just her villa.'

That would be a laughable defence if you or I made it. But Crassus was so notorious for his avarice the judge believed him and Crassus was acquitted. (To answer your unspoken question, yes, he got the villa too.)

His rise to political power had one major problem: the general and statesman Pompey the Great (106–48 BC). The politically popular Pompey kept winning wars and that made him a hit with the Roman people, from plebs to patricians.

Then there was the problem of facing down a slave revolt. After all, it was fine for Crassus to approve of revolt as a means to snatching power, but once he *had* power he suddenly executed a volte-face. He loathed servile insurgence. Crassus enlisted his own army to fight the rampant rebels. One small setback occurred when, faced with a skilled enemy, a part of the Roman army threw down their weapons and fled. Crassus reverted to the ancient Roman practice of decimation – one man in ten executed by the other nine. (The lucky executee was chosen by lot. This was one lottery you did not want to win.)

The brutality worked. Spartacus and his slave army were dangerous, but you had a chance; Crassus was deadlier, and a lost lotto was life-ending.

The revitalized army defeated the slave rebellion of Spartacus in 71 BC. It's said that Spartacus fought his way towards Crassus and slew the two centurions guarding the richest Roman but failed and died in the battle. It ought to have brought the acclaim that Crassus craved. But his great rival, Pompey, mopped up the fugitive slaves and got the greatest reception back in Rome – a triumphal ride into the city. Crassus could have had a sort of runners-up medal – an 'ovation' or a triumphal walk into Rome – but took a huff and said he (unlike Pompey) didn't want recognition for beating a bunch of slaves.

Pompey was known as 'The Great'. Crassus sneered, 'Why, how big is he?' (You may assume he was referring to Pompey's private parts? Shame on you.)

Crassus needed an even greater victory to satisfy his vanity. He spent yet more of his wealth on raising a new private army and set off to the east to pick a fight with the Parthians. He was rich in sesterces but poor in brain cells. His campaign would involve Rome in a conflict that would last for 250 years.

Like many truly rich people he came to believe in his own infallibility – the arrogant belief that he knew better than the rest of us. As well as the household spies, he had hired military moles to report on the enemy, which was a sensible move. But then he didn't take heed of his henchmen. Imagine their frustration. His agents said the Parthians used horse archers whose speed would overwhelm the legionaries in their standard Roman formation. Crassus ignored their counsel.

He listened instead to a treacherous client king who advised him to lead his heavy infantry through a desert, far from a water supply. As his spies had predicted, the light, mounted Parthians inflicted huge damage on the Romans. Crassus retreated and left around four thousand of his wounded to burn in the sun or be slaughtered by the enemy.

Now it was the turn of the surviving Roman troops to rebel and insist that Crassus negotiate with the Parthian general. On their way to the truce meeting, one of Crassus's junior officers panicked when he suspected treachery. He initiated a fight in which all the Romans – including Crassus – were slaughtered. The richest Roman was decapitated.

The Parthians, with a less-than-subtle sense of irony, opened Crassus's mouth and poured in molten gold: a symbolic punishment for the man's greed. 'You like riches? Drink your fill'.

ICENI REVOLT – BOUDICA, AD 61

The Roman statesman Seneca (5 BC–AD 65) said, 'For greed all nature is too little.'

And Seneca was around at the time of the Roman invasion of Britain by Claudius in AD 43. Of course, there are several reasons advanced as to why the Romans chose to occupy a damp patch

11

on the edge of the map: power and glory, trade and security. But, silver, gold, lead and iron were an equally good reason. The Roman rulers loved wealth and invading Britain was a commercial enterprise. They put in cash to raise armies and transport, weapons, and infrastructure. They expected a considerable return on their investment.

The other 'cost' of the expedition would be paid in the blood – obviously they projected more native blood than Roman blood but that would be the fault of the natives. They should simply meekly accept the Roman hegemony, allow themselves to serve the empire and avoid bloodshed.

The Romans were greedy, yet they didn't seem to anticipate their victims could be driven by that same deadly sin. It was greed that aroused wrath in the Iceni tribe of East Anglia to shed buckets of Roman blood and (ultimately) British blood.

By AD 61 Nero had taken the imperial reins. If we are to believe his biographers, Nero was the master of murder and madness. Seneca (who warned us about 'greed') had been teenage Nero's tutor then imperial advisor when Nero took the throne. Did this generate a bond between the two? Apparently not. Nero forced Seneca to kill himself. Seneca was implicated, probably falsely, in a plot to assassinate the emperor. Nero ordered him to take his own life. This teacher's-pet-turned-persecutor was the man the British tribes had to accept as their overlord. Many tribes did and paid tribute to him. Nero raised taxes to pay for his extravagant lifestyle – the family funerals that Nero occasioned must have cost a fortune. Yet it was a relatively trivial bit of avarice that led to an outpouring of blood in the revolt of AD 61.

Boudica was queen of the Iceni tribe in East Anglia. She was not a woman to be trifled with. Roman historian Dio Cassius (AD 150–235) said . . .

> She was huge and terrifying with a harsh voice. A great mass of bright red hair fell to her knees: she wore a twisted necklace, and a tunic of many colours, over which was a thick cloak, fastened by a brooch. Now she grasped a spear, to strike fear into all who watched her.

You will notice that Cassius was writing long after the rebellion and Boudica's subsequent disappearance. It's fair to assume that regardless of this fanciful description of her appearance she was a forceful woman. Yet she and her husband, Prasutagus, had submitted to Roman rule, to their mutual benefit. That benefit included access to Roman loans to improve their quality of life. Prasutagus assumed that when he died the loans would be annulled. And why not? He saw the 'loan' as a bribe. Rome was paying for Iceni collaboration. Nero would have profited from a harmonious peace. Yet instead, the loan provoked disharmony and rebellion. Why? Because Nero's greed overrode his common sense.

When Prasutagus died he did a clever-stupid thing and left a Roman will. This will left the Iceni lands and wealth divided between his Iceni daughters and Emperor Nero. It was clever because it aimed to secure the inheritance for his family. It was also stupid because the Romans saw it as a white flag of weakness. Maybe Nero was influenced by the Roman orator Cicero (106–43 BC), who confidently explained that women have 'a weaker intellect' than men.

Nero must have smiled from coiffed locks to coiffed socks and said he would take it all. This was another clever-stupid action. Clever because it enriched and paid his hairdresser's bills. Stupid because he hadn't done a risk-assessment and asked, 'What would be the consequences of my actions?'

The Roman officials in Britain called in the loans, a move that would have bankrupted Boudica and her tribe. Historian Tacitus (AD 56–c. 120) said that when Boudica and her daughters failed to pay up, the officials had them flogged and raped. Dio Cassius simply said the Roman financiers were to blame for the Iceni reaction. To the Romans a rape was an offence against a woman's 'guardian' (hubby or dad) but not against her personally. Boudica and the Iceni took a different view. And their reaction was violent and bloody.

Big Bad Boud and her allies attacked the Roman settlement at Colchester first, massacred the garrison there and turned towards London.

The Londoners were left to the mercy of Boudica's rebels.

London was a trading port at that time, not a Roman military settlement. Not every Briton hated the Romans. A lot of yuppies were rather taken by the Roman lifestyle and Boudica didn't get a tidal wave of support from south of the Thames. Maybe torching the city was her way of making her point to the southern folk. Maybe she wanted to destroy the bridge across the Thames to protect her rear when she turned north to pursue the Roman general Paulinus? Whatever her motive, the outcome was straightforward: London's burning.

It's said that around seventy thousand Romans and their

sympathizers died . . . but again these are Roman estimates, and they had their own reasons for inflating the figures.

The ending was sadly predictable. The Romans finally managed to bring Boudica's hundred thousand warriors to a set-piece battle, somewhere on Watling Street. The outnumbered but heroic Romans (Roman version) faced the wild British barbarian hordes.

Tacitus claimed Boudica made a grand last speech. She said she wasn't a queen fighting for her lost wealth but a Briton fighting for the freedom of her people and that God was on their side. She said . . .

Heaven is on the side of a righteous revenge; one legion which dared to fight has already perished; the rest are hiding or are thinking of running away. They can't resist even the war-cries of so many let alone our charge and our blows. We must win this battle or die. Let the men live as slaves if they want to. I won't.

And of course she didn't live as a slave. Her army faced ten thousand Romans under Paulinus.

Paulinus's speech to the troops was more practical. According to Tacitus he said . . .

Ignore the noise made by these savages. There are more women than men in their ranks. They aren't soldiers – they're not even properly armed. We've beaten them before and, when they see our weapons and feel our spirit, they'll crack.

Bring them down with your javelins and finish them off with your swords.

The Roman army dutifully obeyed. Paulinus chose a narrow battlefield (somewhere in the Midlands) so the Brits couldn't use their numerical advantage. The Romans used a wedge formation to drive the Britons back to where their own families and followers had formed an arc of supply wagons. The trapped tribes were slaughtered: eighty thousand of them died to only four hundred Romans. Result.

Boudica is then lost to history. Paulinus exacted revenge. His massacres probably killed more than Boudica had done. His diligence in killing off all opposition led to him being relieved of his command by Nero and recalled to Rome under a cloud. Nero's illogical response was, 'Thanks, Paulinus, let's reward you with a slapped wrist.'

Nero had half a dozen years to ruminate on his decision to rob Boudica. He was condemned to death by the senate and took his own life just as he had ordered his old teacher Seneca to do. Neat.

Countless thousands died in the revolt of the Iceni because Nero wanted Boudica's piddling half of a native tribe's wealth. Greed.

NORMAN CONQUEST REVOLT – HEREWARD THE WAKE, 1067

The Battle of Hastings in 1066 was a seminal moment in British history, as you know. Or maybe you don't know. A survey of a thousand British adults in 2024 revealed that a quarter couldn't name the year in which the Battle of Hastings was fought. If you 'tut' at them then you may be apoplectic to hear that 3 per cent believe it was won by Robin Hood and 2 per cent think it was won by Napoleon.*

So, for the avoidance of confusion, William the Conqueror led his Norman troops to victory over Harold II at the Battle of Hastings in 1066. Less familiar is the history of the aftermath and the story of the English who resented the Norman invasion and attempted to reverse it. Like Boudica, they are portrayed as freedom fighters struggling against the invaders. By the English Civil Wars of the 1640s the idea of a 'ruling class' had become known as 'the Norman yoke'.

The original Saxon rebels who had survived the Battle of Hastings (in 1066, lest you forget) were fuelled by the loss of their comfy ruling-class lives. They had been dispossessed of land and property and wanted them back. This sounds more like self-interest than a heroic and patriotic cry of 'Let my people go.'

The regions in the south of England had lost more of their English lords at the Battle of Hastings than those further north. The leaderless southron folk surrendered more readily. After Hastings the Normans approached Winchester and the city rolled over faster than a barrel of wine on a ski slope. The monkish chronicler William of Malmesbury (c. 1095–1143) moaned that, after the Norman Conquest, England became a residence

---

* The 'questions' for the survey were compiled by ten-year-olds who DID know the answers. If you knew those facts then congratulations; you can be reassured you will do well in your Key Stage 2 SATs exams.

for foreigners and that there were no English earls. That wasn't true, but William the Conqueror did redistribute the land extensively to his loyal Norman pals. That helped ensure the new king's hold on the land, but it also helped line his pockets (if his chain-mail had pockets).

The *Anglo-Saxon Chronicle* took the Anglo-Saxon line in reporting the Norman depredations: 'The king and the principal men greatly loved gold and silver and did not care how sinfully it was got as long as it came to them. The king granted his land on such hard terms, the hardest he could.' The chronicle went on to say he offered estates to someone willing to offer an extortionate fee, but then 'the king let it go to the man who offered him more. Then a third came and offered yet more, and the king let it go into the hands of the man who offered him most of all.' He was just like Dickens's Ebenezer Scrooge: 'a squeezing, wrenching, grasping, scraping, clutching, covetous, old sinner'.

William's reign started badly when coronation cheers from inside Westminster Abbey were interpreted by Norman guards outside as a Saxon rebellion. They responded by setting nearby buildings alight. The English spectators ran towards the blaze to courageously douse the flames or equally courageously loot the flaming buildings. The monk Orderic Vitalis (1075–c. 1142) said the whole episode had 'the English believing there was a plot behind something so completely unlooked for, were extremely angry and afterwards held the Normans in suspicion, judging them treacherous'.

The dispossessed Saxons led rebellions but lacked the unity to succeed. The Normans held power with the help of collaborators and quislings. Who can blame them given the Conqueror's reputation. In the siege of Alençon, almost twenty years before, William had ordered that the hands and feet of thirty-two citizens be cut off. Alençon's neighbouring towns quickly surrendered and it became a Norman terror tactic. In the 1075 'Revolt of the Earls' in England, William's commander Geoffrey de Montbray pronounced that all rebels should have their right foot cut off. The rebels hot-footed it from the battlefield while they still had two feet to be hot.

William the Conqueror's principal tactic against the Saxon uprisings had been to build castles in strategic places and garrison them with his troops. Any dissent was then crushed with ruthless slaughter, wasting the land and killing the animals that the locals subsisted on. His 'Harrying of the North' in the winter of 1069–70 was effectively a genocide that left vast areas of England depopulated. It is said that William confessed his regret for that brutality on his deathbed ...

I have persecuted the inhabitants beyond all reason.
Innumerable multitudes, especially in the County of York,
perished through me by famine or sword. I fell upon the
English of the northern shires like a ravening lion. I became the
barbarous murderer of many thousands, both young and old.

He omitted to mention that he had no compunction about looting the monasteries, which had acted as bankers for the former Saxon lords. But as Orderic recorded, the 'foreigners grew wealthy with the spoils of England while her own sons were either shamefully slain or driven as exiles to wander helplessly through foreign kingdoms'.

Faced with such tyranny it is understandable that the rebels wanted to present a moving target rather than a sitting duck. Step forward Hereward the Wake, who chose to stay and fight rather than wander helplessly abroad. Hereward's band of disinherited rebels came up with a novel strategy: they would plunder a monastery themselves. And their excuse for this rapacity towards their own pious people? Glad you asked. They were going to rob the monastery in Peterborough before the Normans could.

They might have looked like chancers taking advantage of the anarchy left in the aftermath of the Harrying of the North, but maybe they were patriotic at heart. So that's all right. Mug a monk as God smiles down on you. Hereward also offered a share of the loot to some Danish mercenaries for their help in the raid.

Hereward's men arrived and burnt down the monastery and most of the peasant homes around it. They were collateral damage. One monk called Ivar was a bit of a boot-licker ... or maybe a sandal-licker. He tried to rescue some of the less valuable gospel books and vestments, which he planned to present to the new abbot. We are not surprised to learn that abbot was Norman and in our own times Ivar would be vilified as a 'collaborator'. Ivar hoped to win himself brownie points on Earth and a free pass into heaven at a later date. We pray that he made it.

Nevertheless, the raiders took a gold diadem from the Great Crucifix and the gold footrest from the feet of the crucified.* The silver and gold altar frontals were plundered, as well as good old cash and the relics of saints. William of Malmesbury had no

---

* I am sure you didn't know that Jesus was crucified with a footrest for comfort, did you?

doubt that Hereward was a small-time thief rather than a hero of the resistance. Will would have been rubbing his ink-stained hands in glee when he wrote that Hereward entrusted the treasure to his Danish chums who promptly ran back to Denmark with the lot. (That was the Danish plan, anyway. Storms drove many of them to seek shelter in Norway or Ireland. Call it divine retribution.)

Hereward and his rebels retreated to fortify the Isle of Ely near Cambridge, as it was secure behind rivers and marshes that were better than any moat. Other Saxon rebels joined him there and William sent an army to defeat them. The legends surrounding Hereward's actions echo the gilded stories of Alfred the Great or Robin Hood (who did NOT win the Battle of Hastings).

One tall tale says Hereward cut his hair and beard and slipped into the Norman camp where he overheard the leaders making their plans. Hereward was recognized and questioned but released on the grounds that he was 'too short' to be the English rebel. Another tale claims the Normans hired a witch to terrorize Hereward's men. (Not a conventional Norman tactic.) The witch (allegedly) stood on a wooden tower facing Hereward's Ely camp and screamed curses and spells before ending by baring her backside towards the rebels. The rebels set fire to her tower, which was the end of that brief spell.

A final story said Hereward was betrayed by a monk of Ely (for a rich reward, naturally) and the Saxon rebel was forced to flee his secure Fenland fortress. It's said he eventually agreed to pay homage to William in return for getting his old family land back. Whichever way you turn – Danish robbers, bribed monks or a hero selling out – it's all about greed.

REBECCA RIOTS OF WALES – THE MORGAN BROTHERS, 1842

*'Cyfiawnder a charwyr cyfiawnder ydym ni oil.'**

BANNER OF PROTEST MARCHERS
IN NEWCHURCH, WEST WALES

Money-motivated revolts aren't always about the money but about the principle. Last week your pack of cigarettes cost £15. Next year it will be £16. It's not the payment you object to but the fact you are paying more for the same thing. (This is quite apart from interfering with your basic human right to kill yourself and your loved ones.) It stands to reason that you are revolting.

That was the mentality of peasant farmers of West Wales in the late 1830s. They were being asked to pay for something that was becoming ruinously expensive: travel.

If you own a piece of land then there are many ways you can make a profit from it. But charging people to cross your land is one of the less popular revenue streams you can generate. If you are an English absentee landowner in Wales then you are already unpopular, aren't you? Charging people to traverse your Welsh tracts of land could spark riots among the hard-working locals.

The peasant farmers of West Wales had a lot of grievances in the early 1840s. The tithes (a tenth of their income) went to the Church of England, even though a significant portion

---

* You don't need me to tell you that this Welsh banner meant 'Justice, and lovers of justice are we all.'

22

of the population in South Wales belonged to Nonconformist Protestant denominations (like Methodism). Many farmers felt they were financially supporting a church they didn't attend.

Then there was the Poor Law Amendment Act of 1834, enacted by those blokes in London that punished the poorest. It was seen as punitive towards the poorest in Wales, including farmers. The act prescribed workhouses as the primary source of state aid for the impoverished. Workhouses offered harsh conditions, separated families, and demanded hard work for miserable rations. The aim of the act wasn't to care for the poor but to deter them from seeking relief. 'Hey, pauper, if you think your life is bad at home then you ought to try the workhouse. You ain't seen nothing yet.' The rural Welsh suffering bad harvests or illness saw this as punishment for bad luck.

'Outdoor relief' (help given outside a workhouse) had been offered to supplement income and allow the poor to stay at home. But this was withdrawn in many parishes. 'Workhouse or nothing' was the rule for many. That injustice was famously highlighted in the popular theatrical monologue 'Christmas Day in the Workhouse', a fictional tale of an old man whose wife was too proud to enter the workhouse. The parish refused 'outdoor relief', so she died. The old man went back to rage against the workhouse governors. It is a wonderful parody of the Victorian taste for mawkish sentimentality, written by George R. Sims (1847–1922), an English satirist, yet it still has the power to evoke the mood of the age as the old man describes his wife's fate:

23

Then she rose to her feet and trembled,
And fell on the rags and moaned,
And, 'Give me a crust, I'm famished . . .
For the love of God,' she groaned.

I rushed from the room like a madman
And flew to the workhouse gate,
Crying, 'Food for a dying woman!'
And the answer came, 'Too late.'
They drove me away with curses;
Then I fought with a dog in the street
And tore from the mongrel's clutches
A crust he was trying to eat.

It was an attack on the rich who gave charitably to the poor, but only in the framework of rigid rules and with a lot of condescension.

Yes, there in a land of plenty,
Lay a loving woman dead,
Cruelly starved and murdered
For a loaf of the parish bread.

The poem was meant as an entertaining music-hall joke at the expense of the straight-faced, strait-laced poetasters and doggerel writers of the time, like Tennyson. Yet George Sims was astounded to discover – late in life – that his humour was treated as a serious piece of anti-Poor-Law propaganda. He said . . .

'Christmas Day in the Workhouse' was for a time vigorously denounced as a mischievous attempt to set the paupers against their betters, but when a well-known social reformer died recently I read in several papers that he always declared that it was reading 'Christmas Day in the Workhouse' which started him on his ceaseless campaign for old age pensions, a campaign which he lived to see crowned with victory.

This is what you, the English landowner, failed to understand when you imposed a toll to cross your estate: the passionate hatred of the ruling classes and the Poor Laws. The theory behind toll roads was fine: travellers pay a toll to walk, ride or drive along a road and, in return, the toll money goes to pay for that road's maintenance. But by 1839 the toll rights were taken over by English fat cats and the profits diverted into their fat purses. At the same time the roads were allowed to deteriorate.

Even to this day potholes are seen as an issue worthy of inclusion in political party promises. In 2023 the Conservatives said they'd set aside £8.3 billion to fill potholes and resurface roads. (The catch? It would be spread over an eleven-year time frame.) Labour said it 'would fix one million extra potholes a year'. What? Personally? Seeing Labour MPs in donkey jackets driving steamrollers would be an entertainment, though I haven't spotted one yet.

The Welsh took to avoiding the toll-gates by taking side roads. The toll owners responded by building 'side-bars': toll-gates on the minor roads to catch anyone trying to dodge the main road tolls. The English absentee toll-owners upped the charges of the side-bars to the fury of the natives, who were paying for something that used to be free.

By the winter of 1842 the sporadic protests had been organized into a movement the rioters called 'The daughters of Rebecca'. They took the name from a verse in the Bible: 'And they blessed Rebekah and said unto her, "Thou art our sister, be thou the mother of thousands of millions, and let thy seed possess the gate of those which hate them."' (Genesis 24:60) 'Possessing the gates' of the toll-bars was the aim. A campaign of criminal damage was planned that could have resulted in the rioters wearing a hangman's rope around the neck. The men's scaffold-dodging tactic was to dress as women and blacken their faces with soot or wear masks.

First the locals destroyed one of the sneaky side-bars by the Mermaid Tavern near St Clears. By the summer of 1843 the Rebecca ranks had swelled to two hundred and this formidable force dismantled the Bolgoed toll-gate near Pontarddulais and damaged the toll-house. The action was the first time a toll-gate had been demolished and gained widespread publicity. Suddenly the riots were significant news. Three men were transported to Australia which only served to pour petrol on the fire of the Welsh anger. Toll-gate wrecking spread across Wales. The Bolgoed incident was led by Daniel Lewis, who called himself 'Rebecca'. He was one of the men transported to Australia where there were no toll-gates to rage against but plenty of sheep to make the Welshmen feel at home.

The riots escalated. William Rees, toll collector of Trevaughan Turnpike Gate, believed he was safe inside his tollbooth. But the rioters wanted to get to his records so they could destroy the names of the people who failed to pay. Rees was tricked into leaving his tollbooth. The report said . . .

> That between one and two o'clock on Sunday morning last he
> was disturbed by a man knocking at his door who enquired
> the way to Llanvallteg Bridge, which he told him and that
> immediately afterwards he heard the sound of horses,
> when about twenty five or thirty men disguised, (having
> white frocks on and their heads tied on with coloured
> handkerchiefs under their chins) came to his house and
> compelled him by threats, pointing at the same time three
> Guns at his breast to deliver up his Books, which they carried
> off. The Books contained among other accounts, the names of
> several persons who had refused to pay toll at the said Gate.
> He is unable to identify any of them, but the person nearest
> to his house window rode a grey horse.

It was only a matter of time before someone died and the unfortunate first was a toll-gate keeper, Sarah Williams. She tried to defy the wreckers but was shot dead. She was killed at the Hendy Gate toll-house in Pontarddulais, Wales.

Rioters suffer human weakness the same as the rest of us. And young local John Jones fell madly in love with one of the rioters' girlfriends. Jones, also known as Johnny of Big Barn, was a petty criminal and a Rebecca rioter. He decided that if he got her boyfriend arrested, he could make the young woman Mrs Jones. So he ran to the constables and betrayed the rioters. He named Henry Morgan of Cwm Cile Farm, north of Swansea, as one of the 'daughters of Rebecca', and Captain Napier, the chief constable, duly took an inspector and two constables to the Morgan farm. There, they met with an unforeseen problem.

It was a Sunday. The devout family were horrified at the idea of the son being taken away on the Sabbath and refused to give him up. In the struggle, Captain Napier was assaulted by the ladies of the house, who threw their scalding breakfast porridge at him. In retaliation Napier shot one of the sons, John Morgan, in the leg, before beating a porridge-covered retreat. They soon returned with reinforcements and took the whole family to Swansea jail. The charge was 'causing an affray'. Two brothers and a sister were jailed for a year.

The other two Morgan brothers faced the more serious charge of rioting. That meant deportation to Australia. Yet they escaped this harsh punishment. The lovelorn informant John Jones was too afraid to testify. His neighbours had given him such a tough time he took himself off to Australia and failed to appear in court. John Jones's brother swore to the police that he could not possibly have witnessed the riot at Rhyd-y-Pandy on that night. The traitor Johnny Big Barn was betrayed by his own family. To make the case for the prosecution worse, the porridge-plastered Captain Napier was shown to be an unreliable witness. He claimed to have been badly injured by the Morgans but was seen playing cricket for Swansea Cricket Club the week after the arrests. The scorecard should have read: 'Captain Napier – caught out.'

The Morgan brothers went free. However, the rioters' cause suffered a great and unexpected blow: a criminal gang started using the Rebecca disguises to hide their felonious and burglarious activities. The gang were caught and transported, but by that time, the devout Nonconformist farmers and peasants felt tainted by association with the thugs.

Yet, before they disbanded and put away their soot-stained dresses, the Rebecca rioters achieved change. The exploitation of the fat cats was stamped out by law from a nervous government and many of the Welsh grievances were addressed.

A descendant of the Morgans commented wryly on the escape from transportation, 'My ancestor . . . was arrested and nearly transported to Australia, so I might have been Bruce Morgan, the premier of New South Wales.' That descendant was Rhodri Morgan (1939–2017), first minister of Wales from 2000 to 2009.

Time is a great healer, they say. So, if you are descended from William the Conqueror don't worry . . . one day the children of the harried north may forgive you. But don't count on it.

LESSONS FROM HISTORY 1
GET A LEADER

*'I am not afraid of an army of lions led by a sheep;
I am afraid of an army of sheep led by a lion.'*
ALEXANDER THE GREAT (356–323 BC) – LEADER

This is not a self-help book on how to be revolting. But
in the event of your ever feeling compelled to dissent,
it is informative to look back at some of the techniques
employed by your predecessors. If tomorrow you need
tips on revolting skills then you can look to yesterday for
inspiration.

Leaders are usually remembered more than the men and
women who fight and die for their cause. The good ones
inspire and share the risks with the followers. The really
good ones are planners who select the battles they can win.

It is possible for a leader to die for the cause and for
that revolution to succeed. You don't really find out how
good a leader is till your revolt is over . . . when you are
cheered as you and your rebels are crowned with laurels,
or jeered as the rope is placed around your neck on the
scaffold. The trouble is that every leader in history – the
winners and the losers – have shared the same weakness:
they are human.

RED EYEBROWS REBELLION – CHINESE PEASANTS, AD 17

Natural disaster was how the AD 17 rebellion in China originated. If anyone were to blame it would be Mother Earth, but She wasn't explaining why She changed the course of the Yellow River between AD 2 and 11. The change led to floods and the floods led to famine. The famine soon led to disease, and the desperate peasants were stuck together with that powerful adhesive: shared misery. The aristocratic target for the misery was the ruling Xin dynasty (AD 8–23).

If they were motivated by hunger then they were inspired by an avenging mother. Mother Lü's son was a minor civil servant who was executed for a trivial offence. Mother Lü was a wealthy landowner who sold her land to pay and equip an army of peasants. She captured the magistrate who had sentenced her son, had him beheaded and offered his head as a sacrifice on her son's grave.

Then she turned her attention on the emperor, a usurper called Wang Mang. His new policies had been an attack on landowners like Mother Lü, so she had extra motivation to depose him. Mother Lü fell ill and died, but other rebels united and took up the cause. These rebel forces were said to have used mediums to communicate – claiming they received messages or guidance from dead heroes. This spiritual leg-up would inspire and legitimize the forces. It was a sign that their gods were on their side.

31

The emperor tried increasing taxes to boost his own army. It was not a clever move to raise taxes for people who were already starving. (HMRC take note.) The Xin emperor sent a massive force of a hundred thousand men to crush the rebels. The rebel leader, Fan, was worried that his men would not be able to tell friend from foe in the heat of battle. He instructed his warriors to paint their eyebrows red. And so the Red Eyebrows united under a common appearance, which had the added advantage of looking fearsome.

By AD 23 they had killed the emperor Wang Mang, so Mother Lü could rest easy in her grave – with no dead head decorating her tombstone, it must be said. But eventually internal squabbling split the Red Eyebrow factions – they didn't see eyebrow to eyebrow. By then the famine had passed and the peasants were more interested in cultivating food on their recovered lands.

JOAN OF ARC (c. 1412–31)

Joan is a rarity in that she died but her revolution succeeded. France was dominated by the English and the nominal French leader, Charles VII, was impotent against their power. He was a defeatist until a shepherdess called Joan said she wanted to meet him. The seventeen-year-old had a direct line to heaven via three angels and they had told her to lead the fightback. Charles VII agreed to see her but put a substitute on the throne and disguised himself among the courtiers. Joan spotted the ruse immediately, approached Charles in the crowd of courtiers and said, 'God give you a happy life, sweet King.' That was enough for Charles to give her a shot at inspiring his demoralized armies.

Against all the odds it worked. Joan may well have been hallucinating about the chatty angels, but the important thing is the French believed her and were motivated. Firstly, her army raised the English siege of Orléans and went on to crown Charles VII as king. And as well as passing on encouragement from the angels, Joan also led by example and put her life on the line. At Orléans she was struck by an arrow in the shoulder but rallied the troops and carried on fighting. An ideal leader.

Of course, it all went pear-shaped when she was captured and handed over to the English. They couldn't execute her for war crimes, that just wasn't sporting. They passed her to a religious court where she was tried for the heinous crime of wearing men's clothing, against the laws of God. The English didn't like the idea that God was on the French side. They had to 'prove' Joan was actually working for the Devil instead and the only 'crime' they could come up with was that wearing men's clothing was an abomination before God. She was sentenced to spend her life in prison.

Three days later she was back in men's clothes, possibly forced to wear them by guards stealing her female clothes. It was a choice between men's clothes and nakedness, and she chose the trouser option. The tribunal condemned her for 'lapsed heresy' – two strikes and you're out. She was handed over to a secular court (because good holy men didn't execute people, you understand). Then she was burnt at the stake. She was only nineteen years old.

She may have died horribly, but the impetus she had generated for the French fightback led to their ultimate victory twenty-two years after her death. Henry V may have won battles like Agincourt, but a peasant woman won the war. That's the sort of leader you need.

What did King Charles VII of France do to save the girl who had given him his crown and France its freedom? Nothing. No ransom, no rescue, no bargaining with the English. He let them burn her. That's not the sort of leader you need.

JACK CADE (1420/30–50)

Almost certainly, the peasants of England were disgusted with the gentry for losing the Hundred Years' War with France. A hundred years of sacrifice for nothing and at the end of it, England faced the threat of invasion from the old foe.

There was an English defence force in the southern counties to deal with the threat, but they were poorly equipped and supplied. It's no surprise that they took to helping themselves to the stores from the towns. They were looting the very people they were supposed to be defending. The government did nothing; indeed, they punished the people. When the corpse of the King's close ally, the Duke of Suffolk, was washed up on the shore at

Dover, the King blamed the people of Kent and they faced reprisals.

All the malcontents needed was a leader and one emerged by the name of Jack Cade. Unlike Joan of Arc his origins are shrouded in mystery, and he was not a saintly martyr, he was a thug. One theory is he was a fugitive from Ireland (or Sussex) where he was accused of murdering a pregnant woman. Or he may have been the son-in-law of a Surrey squire, or he may have just posed as that when he returned from hiding in France. Most prefer the idea he was from the underclasses because it fits the story better.

When the grumbling started, Cade appointed himself 'Captain of Kent' and adopted the alias 'John Mortimer'. The name 'Mortimer' was a sinister challenge to King Henry VI because Henry's main rival for the throne of England was Richard, Duke of York, who had Mortimer ancestry. It was a clever move because it assured the support of a powerful faction of discontented England. York himself was in exile in Ireland at the time – Cade would be the maypole around whom the Yorkists could dance till he returned.

Cade's men from south-eastern England marched on London in order to redress the wrongs done to them. They had success at first, defeating a royal army at Sevenoaks, Kent. Then they marched on to London where the rebels executed the hated lord treasurer, James Fiennes. What use is a dead head if it's buried? Fiennes's head was stuck on a pike and carried aloft through the streets of London. His son-in-law, William Crowmer, also lost his head. What can you do with a pair of heads? They were displayed pushed together as if kissing as they were hoisted onto London Bridge.

It didn't amuse the citizens of London. They were far too upset by the rebels taking the opportunity to loot the city. And Cade joined in the looting. Maybe not the brightest thing to do.* The very people who had been sympathetic to the revolt now turned against the rebel rabble. The Londoners forced Cade's army out of the city in a bloody battle on London Bridge. Cade fled but was later caught on 12 July 1450 by Alexander Iden, a future high sheriff of Kent. In a skirmish with Iden, Cade was wounded and died before reaching London for trial. That inconvenience didn't stop the lords having Cade's body hanged, having his guts cut out and burnt, his head removed, and his body cut into quarters. Unlike his treasury victims, Cade had no one to kiss.

ROBERT ASKE (1500–37) – THE PILGRIMAGE OF GRACE

When Tudor king Henry VIII was bored with his first wife, Catherine of Aragon, the Pope refused to grant him a divorce. If the head of the Catholic Church wouldn't let him have his cross little foot-stamping way then Henry would set up his own church, make himself the head of

---

* As upstanding citizen of Russia Vladimir Putin once put it, 'Those who fight corruption should be clean themselves.'

it and grant his own divorce. He didn't need a consensus. This wasn't some sort of democracy. He would lead his own rebellion against the Catholic Church but call it a 'Reformation' rather than a rebellion.

It's not as though the Catholic Church didn't need reforming. Discontent had been spreading through Europe ever since the Czech theologian Jan Hus had died for Protestant reform a hundred years before. But Henry VIII had originally boasted of suppressing Protestants in England. In 1521 Pope Leo X even gave Henry the equivalent of a religious Oscar when he named him 'Defender of the Faith'.

One of the Protestant victims of Henry's Catholic zeal was Anne Askew, the only woman to be tortured on the rack in the Tower of London. The lord chancellor, Richard Rich, and the Earl of Southampton weren't afraid to get their hands dirty and worked the rack themselves, slowly stretching her arms and legs apart. Anne said: 'Master Rich the torturer put me on the rack till I was nearly dead . . . When I was set loose I fainted. They woke me up and then put me on the rack again.'

She refused to name her fellow Protestants. Anne was stretched so much she couldn't walk. Instead, she was carried out of the Tower to Smithfield, where she was burnt alive along with two others. A report said . . .

> And thus the good Anne Askew, having passed
> through so many torments, having now ended the
> long course of her agonies, being compassed in with

flames of fire, as a blessed sacrifice unto God, she slept in the Lord AD 1546, leaving behind her a singular example of Christian constancy for all men to follow.

JOHN FOXE — ENGLISH MARTYROLOGIST,
ACTES AND MONUMENTS

John Foxe wrote that gunpowder was used to 'rid her of her pain'. But another account said that the execution lasted about an hour and that Anne was most likely unconscious after about fifteen minutes. Was the gunpowder ineffective? Whatever the truth, the spectators were impressed by Anne Askew's bravery, by the fact that she didn't cry out or scream in pain until the flames reached her chest. She died the same way she had lived, with fortitude. An inscription on her portrait reads: 'Rather death than false of faith.'

Anne may have been a martyr, but she wasn't a leader. The job of leading a major Catholic uprising against Henry's Protestant Reformation fell to Robert Aske. He was born in Selby in Yorkshire but working in London as a barrister when revolt broke out. The tipping point had been Henry's closure of the monasteries, and the uprising became known as 'The Pilgrimage of Grace'. Aske went north to join the pilgrimage and soon became its leader.* He had the sincerity and passion of Joan of Arc coupled with the charisma and eloquence of Jack Cade.

---

* Aske had only one eye, so he was never going to see eye to eye with Henry.

The pilgrims' demands were clear and reasonable – that the closing of monasteries should stop, Henry's Catholic daughter Mary Tudor should be named as his heir and the power of the Pope should return to England.

Their chances of success were quite realistic compared to previous revolts. Henry had no standing army ready to confront the riots. When Robert Aske led the protests in Pontefract in the north, they weren't a warlike group. These Pilgrims carried banners and wore badges that showed the bleeding wounds of Christ – but they weren't bloodthirsty. In fact, they were ordinary men and women who wanted to protest peacefully.

Some of Aske's pilgrims planned to march to London to persuade Henry in person, but Aske refused to let them, saying they were a Holy group and not a rioting mob. He insisted they could prevail while preserving King Henry and his family but driving out all wicked advisers and ministers. Sometimes you can be too reasonable.

Henry needed to buy time to raise an army, so he responded with guile by telling them, 'Look, lads, you go home peacefully, and I'll look at your complaints. I will also pardon you . . . as long as you make no more trouble.' The victorious petitioners went home, pleased that everything was going well.

Unfortunately, some peasants then attacked Carlisle, claiming it was in the name of the Pilgrimage of Grace (which it wasn't). That gave Henry the excuse he was looking for to unleash his new army and give the chilling order to the Duke of Norfolk: 'Cause such dreadful executions upon a good number of the inhabitants hanging them on trees, quartering them, and setting the quarters in every town, as shall be a fearful warning.'

Naturally the cowardly king selected soft targets. Places like Sawley Monastery had been re-opened by the pilgrims – Henry's men took the monks and hanged them from the steeple of the church so everyone could see what happened to rebels.

Aske was invited to meet Henry – under the promise of safe passage, naturally – so he could spend Christmas as a guest of the King. If the saintly pacifist Aske had a weakness as a leader then it was that he was too trusting. Would you go and meet the King – as Wat Tyler had 155 years before? Did Robert Aske even study the history of the Peasants' Revolt in school? Apparently not.

We bury your heads in our hand and sob, 'Don't do it, Robert.' But he did.

Friendly Henry wanted the names of all these good pilgrim leaders. Aske, the loyal subject, gave them. Aske was then arrested, tried and sentenced to death for high treason, with no Christmas pudding. In June 1537 he was taken back to York after being paraded through the northern towns and villages. Aske was executed in front of the people who had followed him. He was hanged from the walls of York Castle in chains and left to die slowly and in agony. An example to any would-be rebels. '*Pour encourager les autres*,' as the fluent French-speaking king may have chuckled.

It's said that Aske's servant, Robert Wall, died of grief

at the thought of his master's execution. But Henry had just started his reign of terror. Under the guise of 'martial law' Henry's ministers conducted massacres in as public a way as possible. Further priests, monks and abbots were hanged from their church steeples. More than two hundred ordinary men were hanged from their roofs or trees in their own gardens while their families looked on.

Robert Aske would be the ideal sort of leader for any revolt you were planning except for one weakness: he was naive.

WHAT'S IN A NAME?

If you are going to have a leader then get one with a suitably upbeat name. If they don't have one then invent one. History has had a mix of the brilliant and the bizarre . . .

- HAMMERER. In 165 BC the Syrians ruled the Jews in Jerusalem. Then a Jewish leader called Judas rose to lead them in rebellion. He was given the name 'Maccabeus', a Hebrew name which means 'Hammerer'.

- SHEDDER OF BLOOD. In AD 750 Abu'l-abbas led a revolution in Mesopotamia and killed the royal family, the Umayyads. His followers gave him the name al-Saffah, which means 'Shedder of Blood'.

- SLAYER OF BULGARS. Basil was Byzantine emperor from 976 to 1025. He defeated the Bulgarian army in the year 1014 and took most of their soldiers alive then gave the gory order: 'I want the eyes of almost every soldier to be put out. One Bulgarian in a hundred must be allowed to keep a single eye so he can lead his friends back home.' The Bulgarian ruler, Tsar Samuel, took one look at his eyeless army and dropped dead from the shock. Basil was given the name Bulgaroctonus. Slayer of the Bulgars. Strictly speaking it should have been 'Blinder of the Bulgars'.

- THE DRAGON. The Turkish army invaded Transylvania in 1462 but reckoned without the Transylvanian prince Vlad Tepes, who led the rebellion against the invaders. The name given to him for his cruel torture of prisoners was Vlad the Impaler, which isn't a bad name in itself. But 'Dragon' in Romanian was Dracul and Vlad became the legendary Dracula.

- SAUCE THE GROCER. When the French king and queen tried to escape the revolution in 1791, Monsieur Sauce, a local grocer and magistrate, held the runaways and sent them back to Paris for the chop. Chops are better with Sauce.

- JOAQUIM THE DENTIST. This Brazilian freedom fighter led his people in the 1780s against the Portuguese occupiers. He was also an expert dentist and nicknamed 'Tiradentes' or 'Tooth-puller'. His revolution failed and he was the only one executed, hanged and cut into pieces – a fate that many odontophobes may wish on their own drillers and fillers.

- RAIN-IN-THE-FACE. This Sioux warrior was captured by the Seventh Cavalry and escaped. His captor was Tom Custer, the younger brother of the famous general. A legend says that when Rain-in-the-Face escaped he swore he would return and eat Tom Custer's heart. At the Battle of the Little Bighorn in 1876, Rain-in-the-Face finally met up with Tom again . . . and kept his promise. Or has this been lost in translation and did he actually eat a custard tart?

REASON TO REVOLT 2
REVENGE

'It is impossible to suffer without making someone pay for it; every complaint already contains revenge.'
FRIEDRICH NIETZSCHE (1844–1900) – GERMAN
PHILOSOPHER

Revenge is a very unworthy motive. It is also very satisfying. Someone makes you suffer so you strike back in the best way you can manage. If it is your oppressor that upsets you then rebellion not only gives you the opportunity to free yourself but also the chance to inflict pain on someone who has meted it out on you.

JULIUS MARTIALIS – ASSASSINATION OF CARACALLA, AD 217

'Taking the law into your own hands' is generally perceived as a pejorative comment. The law will protect you and – when it fails – the law will avenge you. But what if the law conspires to protect the guilty? What if the guilty are the law, and the only way to get 'justice' is to take revenge?

In Imperial Rome, Geta was the younger brother of Caracalla. The brothers had ruled jointly with their dad, Septimius Severus, for a while. When the old man departed the marbled stage then Geta and Caracalla were meant to rule jointly, but after two fractious years they decided they didn't like sharing. They physically divided the palace and bricked up (or marbled up) any doorways between their halves. On 25 December 211 Caracalla suggested a meeting. Geta was suspicious but was reassured that their mother, Julia Domna, would be there to mediate, and the meeting would take part in her apartments. Geta agreed. He knew that he was mummy's favourite, and she wouldn't let Caracalla harm him.

Out of respect for their mother, Geta left his guards behind when the brothers met. The atmosphere must have been tense, but not for long. On a given signal Caracalla's imperial guards broke into the room. Geta realized he was outnumbered (as well as briefly realizing he'd been out-thought). The twenty-two-year-old little boy ran to his mother's arms. The most ruthless of guards would not see him attacked as he clung to Mum, would they? But they did. He was butchered and died at Julia Domna's bosom. As well as making a mess of her toga this must have been traumatic and something for which antenatal classes hadn't prepared her.

Caracalla held up his innocent hands – 'I never touched him, Ma' – and made the familiar excuse. It was a pre-emptive strike, he said. When you thought about it, it was really a sort of self-defence. I had to kill him because I heard he was plotting to kill me. Geta was too dead to deny this. Not satisfied with deleting Geta, Caracalla then set about expunging his name from stone or papyrus inscriptions as well as destroying portraits. Geta became, in the term coined by George Orwell in his novel 1984, an 'unperson'.

Caracalla knew the Roman tradition was for supporters to avenge the murder of their leader. Again, the pre-emptive tactic was deployed, and he went about exterminating all of Geta's supporters – some reports claim 12,000 died in the purge. But this sort of house-clearing was like the mythical Greek Hydra: every time a head was cut off, two more grew in its place. For every single one of the 12,000 he killed there were families and friends who would vow revenge. In AD 215 he travelled to Alexandria and there he was met by a hostile mob chanting about his brother's murder. That either irritated him or stirred a guilty conscience because he had the hecklers massacred. They in turn had families ... you get the picture. Caracalla couldn't kill everyone in the world, though he was making a decent attempt.

Sooner or later one of the outraged loved ones would find their opportunity. Sir Francis Bacon put it best: 'Revenge is a kind of wild justice ... vindictive persons live the life of witches who, as they are mischievous, so end they infortunate.' After so many executions, the senate were quite relieved when Macrinus, head of the Praetorian Guard, had Caracalla murdered.

There is a story that Macrinus was prophesied to be next emperor. The Romans like prophecies. Spilling the entrails of chickens, and seeing how they fell, was popular. (Though not among chickens.) Macrinus said that the prophecy made him a target for Caracalla. He argued he wouldn't be safe till Caracalla died. So, he had the emperor killed first. That's right – his excuse was that it was a pre-emptive strike. Sometimes irony, like revenge, is sweet.

The man who delivered the fatal blow was Julius Martialis from Caracalla's own bodyguard. The emperor had had Martialis's brother executed a few days before on some sham charge and, as it turned out, Martialis was out for revenge. Yet more irony that Caracalla, the man who had murdered his brother, was killed by Martialis, a man who loved his brother.

What was Caracalla doing having a man with a grudge in his personal bodyguard? Maybe he thought the other guards were so loyal they would protect him. But they failed to keep an eye on him at a critical moment as they rode to the temple of the Moon. Caracalla stopped on the journey to have a pee in a ditch. The other guards turned away politely but the killer lunged forward and killed Caracalla with a single blow. The expression 'caught with his pants down' has never been more relevant.

The guards caught and killed Martialis. The probable instigator, Macrinus, took over, as the prophecy foretold; as is the way of the Roman Empire, he didn't last long.

HARALD HARDRADA AND TOSTIG – STAMFORD BRIDGE, 1066

You wait twenty-four years for a new king then four come along at once.

Edward the Confessor reigned all that time and, when he died in 1066, left a power vacuum. The jackals had been gathering for a while, hoping to dart onto the throne and take the place of the old king.

It was surprising that Edward the Confessor had lasted so long. His family had spent several years in exile in Normandy, so the English nobles didn't trust them. When Ed the Con's younger half-brother Alfred first arrived in England to take the throne he was greeted warmly by the treacherous English nobleman Harold Harefoot. Harefoot invited Alfred to a hilltop to view the kingdom that would be his. It was the last thing Alfred did see because his English escort bound him and put out his eyes with red-hot pokers. He died soon after.

This was the sort of dangerous world Edward eventually inherited. Those twenty-four years of his reign are often portrayed as 'peaceful' but the Normans, the Vikings and the English were just dormant volcanoes waiting to erupt as soon as Edward died. He could have been called Edward the Confuser because he died without clear instructions to say who was the rightful heir. He had no children but there was no firm principle of primogeniture in place in Saxon England anyway. The biggest bully – or the fastest out of the blocks – would claim the prize.

The claimants were:

Edgar Aetheling: He was Ed the Con's nearest relative but he was only fifteen years old so not experienced enough to fight his corner.

Harold Godwinson: He was in pole position in the English court, ready to get a head start as soon as Ed the Con vacated the throne. Would he take the crown? (Spoiler alert: the answer is 'Yes'.)

William, Duke of Normandy: A distant cousin of Edward
who claimed that Edward had promised him the throne
earlier, and that Harold Godwinson had conceded
William's right on a visit to Normandy. Would he invade
to back up his claim? What do you think?

Harald Hardrada: The Norwegian king claimed the throne
based on his ancestors' Viking heritage and he also said
he had inherited a promise made to his family. Would he
invade to enforce his claim? You bet.

Harold Godwinson was first out of the starting blocks and won
the race. He had the crown on his head before it had time to cool.
A couple of the other claimants said they had been promised the
throne and were miffed when it was snatched from under their
snouts. They wanted revenge and they were going to fight for it
or die trying.

Hardrada had an ace up his sleeve: Harold Godwinson's
brother, Tostig, who had been evicted from England over his
rule in Northumbria. The Northumbrian nobles hated Tostig's
brutal actions and had appealed to Ed the Con to remove him.
With Harold Godwinson's advice, Edward had sent Tostig into
exile: a metaphorical stab in Tostig's back.

Tostig was furious and spoiling for a fight to win back his earl-
dom. Yet again brotherly hate motivated the conflict. Exiled and
bitter, Tostig wanted revenge on his brother and a path back to
his power and position. He approached William of Normandy
to make a joint invasion. William said, 'Non,' because of course he
was planning his own European Union and didn't need a chancer
like Tostig on board.

Tostig attempted a few raids on the English coast, but they were feeble and easily repelled. He needed a big, bad Viking ally. He turned to the King of Norway, Hardrada, and offered to support his invasion to put Hardrada on the throne. Tostig's policy seemed to be, 'Anyone but bruv Harold.' It is just possible that Tostig fancied the English throne for himself. Once he and his new best friend Hardrada had defeated brother Harold then Tostig could stab Hardrada in the back – literally.

The stage was set for a family fight between Harold Godwinson and Tostig that would eclipse Cain and Abel's and have the same result – one dead brother.

York was a wealthy centre of Saxon power and capturing it would give the Norwegians a commanding base. It was also too far north for Harold Godwinson to rush to its defence. He was amassing his forces on the south coast anticipating a Norman invasion.

Around 8 September 1066 an army of ten thousand Vikings under Hardrada arrived to conquer the north. This man was said to be Christendom's best warrior. There were 300 longships landed at Riccall on the river Ouse to the south of the city, manned by men from all over the Viking world including large areas of northern England. He had Tostig hanging on to his coat tails. They set up camp and on 20 September they marched on York.

They were met by the English Earls Edwin and Morcar – another pair of brothers – with an army of inexperienced troops who bravely inflicted heavy losses on the invaders until, by the end of a long summer day, they were overwhelmed. Or it may be more graphic to say they were 'swamped' because they were driven into a marshy area where they were cut down. Reports said there were so many bodies the Vikings were able to cross the swamp by stepping on English corpses like stepping stones. Treacherous Tostig's local knowledge probably helped to manoeuvre the English into the mire. At that battle, known as the Battle of Fulford, he'd proved his value to Hardrada.

The victorious Vikings then marched towards York, but Hardrada refrained from pillaging because he didn't want 'his' new capital destroyed. The Vikings took some supplies and a few hostages then retired.

Hardrada sent a message to the people of York. He said that his warriors wanted bread and wine. To prevent the citizens betraying him he asked for 150 children from the wider area of Yorkshire as hostages. They would ensure the north would support his invasion. He told the defeated city his men would collect the supplies and bonus batch of hostages from Stamford Bridge some seven miles east of the city. The folk of York agreed so they were effectually offering home-delivery nine hundred years before supermarkets thought of it. Hardrada gave them till Monday, 25 September to come up with the goods – and the kids.

Now dates in history can be dull and only useful for testing students. But in this case they are significant. The Vikings waited twelve days before confronting the Saxon earls. They now waited another five days after the Battle of Fulford to enter York. Seventeen days. Even by third-class donkey-mail that gave Harold time to receive news of the invasion on 16 September and march north from London. He gathered his troops from the southern defences and set off to hike 190 miles in six days. ('That's more than thirty miles a day if you want to save your abacus.) Harold arrived at York on 24 September 1066. He augmented his footsore army with local militias. His intelligence told him of the Viking hostage collection the next day near Stamford Bridge.

And speaking of intelligence, it's something Hardrada lacked – in both senses. Hardrada may have been Christendom's best warrior, but he wasn't the brightest candle on the Christmas tree. Or maybe he was just over-confident. On 25 September he went to Stamford Bridge to collect his provisions and his hostages. He had less than half of his army and they didn't have all their weapons. It was a warm September day, so they didn't bring all of their armour from their anchorage fifteen miles away at Riccall. They were expecting peaceful citizens of York. Instead, they got King Harold of England and his army. We have no record of his reaction to seeing Harold Godwinson's forces, but it may have been something like, 'Oooops.' Or something a little stronger. Fill in the blanks.

Before the battle was joined, Harold made a generous fraternal offer to his brother Tostig. He suggested Tostig could have a third of the kingdom if he would come over to the Saxon side. That's a bit suspicious, isn't it? Tostig didn't command a significant force and had done nothing to deserve such a huge reward. If you had a nasty, suspicious mind you might think Harold Godwinson planned to kill Tostig as soon as he left the security of the Viking lines?

A messenger carried the offer to Harold Godwinson's brother but Tostig wasn't going to rise to the bait. Instead, he responded with a query, 'What about my ally, Hardrada?'

The messenger came up with the legendary quote that is up

there with Stanley's 'Doctor Livingstone I presume,' or Victoria's 'We are not amused,' or Cnut's 'I've got cold feet.'

The messenger replied, 'Seven feet of English ground, as he is taller than other men.' Macho.

Tostig showed some loyalty and replied that he hadn't brought the King of Norway to England to betray him. The messenger returned to the Saxon host. Hardrada was impressed by the boldness of the messenger and asked Tostig who the cheeky chap was. 'That was my brother Harold,' he said.

A Hollywood scriptwriter couldn't have typed a better scene. It would be nice to think it was true. Whatever the prelude, the battle was engaged.

And what a fight followed. A Viking hero blocked the bridge and killed forty English before they could cross. The English sent a boat under the bridge, pushed a pike through the planks and stabbed him from below. It reached the parts that other armour didn't reach. Ouch. That delay allowed the invaders to form a shield wall. Still their lack of armour put them at a disadvantage.

Harold's men eventually overran the Vikings. Hardrada got his reward of the seven feet of earth that his enemy promised.

Tostig was given a second chance to surrender but refused and was cut down. Reinforcements hurried from the Viking ships at Riccall but in the hot afternoon sun some of the Vikings died of heatstroke. They delayed Harold Godwinson's victory a little while but eventually were broken and fled for their ships.

The English victory was such that only twenty-four longships were needed to get the Viking survivors home. Three days later, before the army could catch its breath, Harold was given the bad news that another challenger for the throne, Duke William the Bastard of Normandy, had landed. A lot is made of the fact that Harold had to march his battle-weary army south again and meet the Normans nineteen days after Stamford Bridge. But here's a thought: 300 longboats brought the Vikings to England. Twenty-four of those longships left with the remnants of Hardrada's army. So . . .

- What happened to the 276 longboats left on the Yorkshire riverbank?
- Why didn't Harold Godwinson commandeer the ships and sail back to London?
- Or did he sail south . . . and have nine hundred years of history books got it wrong?

The weariness of the men who fought at Stamford Bridge is cited as an excuse for Harold losing the subsequent battle on the south coast at Hastings.

This invasion was not unexpected, and the English fleet and local fyrd (militia) had been guarding the south coast all summer. The coming of autumn with its accompanying gales had meant that Harold had dismissed the land forces to let the men help with the harvest. It allowed the English fleet to shelter in harbour. The Normans had indeed suffered from the gales, but William was having difficulties in keeping his mainly mercenary army together so made the most of a lull and crossed the Channel.

Still, Harold had fresh forces in the south. He hit William's Normans by surprise just as he had Hardrada's Vikings. Harold took the higher ground. He held all the cards. He lost. His brother Tostig's revolting revenge attacks didn't help. But were they a major cause of William's conquering victory as the text-books have repeated for close on a thousand years? Or do we need to rewrite history?

IVAYLO – THE BULGARIAN UPRISING, 1280

Sometimes you can get so exasperated by your leaders you need to oust them and replace them. If they are really incompetent, then you may find you have more willing rebels out there than you imagined. In that case it doesn't matter how lowly you are, you can end up in power. Zero to hero.

The Mongols were a ruthless horde of warriors who had raided and looted Bulgaria for decades. The peasants (as usual) bore the brunt of the enemy's incursions – they raised crops and animals only to see them stolen by thugs who didn't want the effort of farming for themselves.

Ivaylo was a swineherd with enough charisma to lead a fightback. In 1277 he gathered an army of malcontents, mainly peasants, and got his revenge against the Mongols who were unaccustomed to such resistance. Not content with beating back the raiders, Ivaylo then led a rebellion against the incompetent aristocrats who ruled his country. He met the Bulgarian tsar Constantine Tikh face to face in battle and killed him in his chariot. This was not quite the heroic victory it sounds because Constantine Tikh had been partially paralysed some years before when he fell from his horse. Still, slaying an emperor is always a good career move. Then the swineherd came up with a better one after his triumphal entry into the capital: he married Tikh's widow, Maria.

We don't know the empress's reaction to marrying a swine-herd, but she must at least have been pleased that her supply of bacon sandwiches was secured. Her reputation was for being sly and manipulative. She was party to a previous emperor being blinded then deposed and another pretender dying from poison; the sort of woman someone like Ivaylo would want onside. Ivaylo became emperor as the heir, Michael Asen II, was a minor.

Naturally the monarchs of the region were shocked by Maria marrying someone of the underclasses who had killed her husband. They said she had 'brought disgrace on the family' and you can hear them huffing with indignation as they said it. The marriage was said to be an unhappy one and Ivaylo was soon engaged in a new battle with the Mongols in 1279. It only took the rumour of Ivaylo's death to panic the nobles into electing a new emperor.

Ivaylo wasn't, in fact, dead and decided on a clever plan to reclaim his imperial throne. In 1280 or 1281, he approached the Mongol leader Nogai Khan with a proposal: 'I'll accept you as my overlord if you help me get my throne back.' Nogai Khan seemed delighted with the idea but pointed out there was a rival to the throne called Ivan. He invited them both to a feast – one on each side of him. Before they'd even reached the pudding course, Ivan jumped up and pointed to Ivaylo, crying, 'He is an enemy of my father, and does not deserve to live.' With the Mongol Nogai Khan's consent the swineherd was killed on the spot – a pork chop.

Malicious Maria went off into exile and the Mongols went from strength to strength. Ivaylo's first Bulgarian Peasants' Revolt ended in failure, as they usually did. Yet, like Wat Tyler in England a hundred years later, the Bulgarian peasant leader is remembered as someone who strove against the odds to overcome the incompetence of the privileged classes. It was a glorious failure that is not forgotten in his homeland. The people there remember their rags-to-riches-emperor and call him Bardokva – 'cabbage' – in memory of his humble beginnings.

MAKE A MARTYR

'Let us all be brave enough to die the death of a martyr but let no one lust for martyrdom.'

MAHATMA GANDHI (1869–1948) – INDIAN LEADER

If you want to win a rebellion then get yourself a martyr. No matter how dubious their reputation in life, they will dazzle with their halo in death . . . until a cynical writer comes along to debunk their myth in what some will call a 'revisionist' history. Not many people have irreproachable lives (except you and me, of course).

SAINT EDMUND OF ENGLAND (AD 841–69)

It may also help if our martyr suffered a particularly unjust punishment and died a painful death. Saint Edmund of England (died AD 869) is remembered as 'Edmund the Martyr'. His Viking captors tied him to a tree and filled him full of arrows, separated his ribs from his spine and pulled out his lungs – a sadistic trick known as the Blood Eagle. After merciful decapitation, his head was thrown into some undergrowth. The loyal Saxon searchers went looking for it. Ed's dead head helped by calling out to them, 'I am here, I am here.' A miracle, and one reason why he became a saint. A king and a saint – there's a rarity.

Edmund's refusal to submit to Viking demands for him to kneel in submission and renounce his Christian faith made him a symbol of faithful Christianity and Saxon resistance against the Viking pagans. A martyr is a totem around which rebels can unite. Everyone agrees that a dead hero or heroine is a potent weapon (unless you're the one being martyred). The Saxons rallied around and fought back in the name of the blessed Edmund. Eventually they drove out the Vikings.

Another bunch of Vikings moved into France in AD 911 and called themselves Normans. They crossed the Channel and conquered England under their Duke William. English autonomy vanished for ever. But it was nice while it lasted. Despite the Norman conquest, Edmund remained patron saint of England until the 1300s when a fictional St George took Edmund's title after he fictionally slew a fictional dragon and rescued a fictional maiden in fictional distress. (We can all do that.)

Here is a strange coincidence: King Edmund was patron saint of 'protection from plagues'. He was elbowed aside by St George in the 1300s, and what happened? The Black Death struck in the middle of the century. Just saying. Clearly King Ed went off in a huff and took his pandemic protection with him.

WENCESLAS OF BOHEMIA (907–35)

Just sixty-six years after Edmund was used as a pincushion by vicious Vikings, the Christian Wenceslas of Bohemia died at the hands of his pagan brother, Boleslaus.

Wenceslas was a practical Christian, setting up charitable centres, and devoted his life to caring for the sick and disabled, widows and orphans. He was a one-man combination of Salvation Army and Dr Barnardo. You could even call him 'Good' King Wenceslas because it scans quite poetically.

His mother Drahomíra was passionate about paganism and purging Christianity. Once Wence inherited at the age of eighteen he packed off his murderous mummy into exile and reversed her paganish persecutions.

He couldn't convert his younger brother, Boleslaus, the Cruel, who led disgruntled lords in rebellion against their king. Wenceslas started paying invading forces to go away rather than resist. The lords didn't like a weak Wence. Two of them stabbed the good king repeatedly and Boleslaus the Cruel finished him off with a lance. He was chopped down at the doors to a church where, naturally, miracles happened thereafter. He didn't do much looking out on the Feast of Stephen after that. He is now patron saint of Czechia. (A 'king' representing a 'republic'? There's another rarity.)

Drahomíra had a track record of murdering relatives. Wenceslas's paternal grandmother was strangled by

Drahomíra's assassins. It seems they didn't go prepared to garotte a granny because they used her own veil to strangle her. It is shocking to think any self-respecting assassin would go to a killing so unprepared. It's practically criminal.

As we know, 'the people's flag is deepest red, it shrouded oft our martyred dead'. Rebels can march behind that blood-red banner – but ideally you should avoid being a martyr yourself or you won't enjoy world domination when it comes.

MARGARET CLITHEROW – CATHOLIC RESISTANCE, 1586

Of all the regimes suffered by the English people, the Tudor family is arguably the most misremembered. If a lazy designer is commissioned to create a visual image of England's historic past then they will usually select a Tudor rose or, worse, the megalomaniac Henry VIII. Heritage sites have been known to hire a portly ginger bloke to wander around and entertain the visitors. Of course, the re-enactor portrays the murderous king Henry VIII as genial and avuncular, and as far from earthly reality as Uranus.

The other popular symbol of England past is his bejewelled daughter, Elizabeth, who inherited his iniquitous sadism yet revels in the title 'Gloriana'. She is even hailed by some modern historians of very little brain as heralding a 'Golden Age'. Really? Like Victoria, she achieved her legendary status by living a long time while avoiding assassins and watching men, women and children die for her peccadilloes.

The weedy Edward VI, the mean and dentally challenged Henry VII and the deranged Bloody Mary aren't such striking poster-posers, so they don't get a look in. Neither do the real heroines and heroes of Tudor England, the martyrs who rebelled against the Tudor totalitarians.

Margaret Clitherow of York was one of Gloriana's 'official' victims – one of nearly two hundred executed under anti-Catholic legislation. (Many other unofficial victims barely trouble the record books as they only suffered imprisonment, exile and torture.) You may assume Margaret's crime was to be a Catholic, and she was, but it wasn't that simple.

You see, Margaret Middleton was two years old when Catholic Queen Mary died in 1558, and Protestant Elizabeth came to the throne. On the religious carousel the English were ordered to switch religions yet again. Alternatively, they could hide their Catholicism. Many, like the Middletons, stayed secret Catholics. Margaret's fate was sealed by her parents at the age of two.

In 1571, fifteen-year-old Margaret married butcher John Clitherow of the Shambles in York and they had three children. John was a Protestant but had a brother who went to train as a Catholic priest in Reims. A death sentence for the butcher's brother if he were caught. The steaks were high.

As it turned out, John Clitherow was responsible for betraying Catholic worshippers in his parish. Awkward. His wife Margaret struggled to worship in the local Protestant church and was imprisoned in 1577 for dodging compulsory church attendance. There would be two more incarcerations for her at York Castle, the second lasting twenty months. She was on the road to martyrdom. In 1583, five Catholic priests were executed at Knavesmire in York (now a racecourse). Yet Margaret went on defiantly holding Catholic masses in her home. A hidden chapel was constructed. She had a hole cut into the adjoining house wall so her guest-priests could escape when there was a raid by the Protestant police.

Margaret was eventually caught in 1586 when her frightened young son revealed the chapel to the Catholic-hunters. So far so predictable. She was taken to court and asked to plead, guilty or not guilty. But there was a catch. If she pleaded guilty she'd be executed . . . but her innocent children would be disinherited and left destitute. If she pleaded not guilty those children (and her loyal servants) would be coerced or even tortured into giving evidence against her.

Her third path was to refuse to plead. She must have known the authorities were wise to that and the consequences were terrible. A law from the 1400s said:

> Such felons as stand mute, and speak not at their
> arraignment, are pressed to death by huge weights
> laid upon a board that lieth over their breast, and a

sharp stone under their backs. And these that held their peace, thereby to save their goods unto their wives and children, if they were condemned, should be confiscated to the prince.

An eyewitness from the same era described the inducement in graphic detail. It hadn't changed much:

> He will lie upon his back, with his head covered and his feet, and one arm will be drawn to one quarter of the house with a cord, and the other arm to another quarter, and in the same manner it will be done with his legs; and let there be laid upon his body iron and stone, as much as he can bear, or more.

Margaret shrugged and said, 'God be thanked, I am not worthy of so good a death as this.' And so she was taken to the bridge over the river Ouse, where a large number of York residents could learn from her example. There was a bit of a delay when the law officers discovered no one wanted the job of pressing her. After a search, three beggars were persuaded to take on the gruesome task.

Margaret was stripped and had a handkerchief tied across her face. The sharp rock placed under her back was supposed to be a mercy – if the weight was too much to bear, it would break her spine and give a quick release. A heavy door was placed over her. Stones were placed on top of the door. Despite the increasing pain she still refused to plead. They loaded the door with rocks and stones weighing at least 700 pounds (320 kg). Death came within fifteen minutes, but her body was left for six hours before the weight was removed.

Margaret is remembered at a shrine in her house in the Shambles, where she lived. But her death poses uncomfortable questions. Firstly, did Margaret 'lust for martyrdom', as Gandhi put it?

Margaret Clitherow certainly chose her death. She has become a martyr, and her tormentors are rightly despised. But reports say she was pregnant at the time – which drops a mine into the moral maze. Did her persecutors murder an innocent unborn? And did Margaret knowingly allow an innocent foetus to die? It's called a moral maze because there is no simple way out for us rats.

Gloriana the Queen (a week or so too late) wrote to the people of York to say Margaret Clitherow should not have been executed. Elizabeth has a track record for this sort of apology. A year later her cousin, Mary Queen of Scots, died on the block. Elizabeth had signed the order but later claimed it was accidental. She reinforced her dismay at the 'accidental' execution by punishing the advisors who took the warrant that she had signed. Believe it if you will.

Did the martyrdom of Margaret spark a rebellion against the Protestant establishment? Not directly. But here is a sensational and original theory that has never been aired before.

- Margaret Clitherow was executed in York in March 1586. (Fact.)

- At that time the city was the home of a sixteen-year-old Protestant boy. (Fact.)

- He could not have avoided the sensation it caused in the city. It is even likely that he had been in the crowd that watched her die so bravely or filed past the corpse as it lay there for six hours. It was one of the busiest bridges in the city.

- Margaret had died at the hands of Protestants acting on behalf of their Protestant queen. It was the sort of shameful act that would taint both church and queen.

- Within five years the boy had converted to Catholicism, and two years after that he was fighting for the Spanish Catholic cause in Europe. (Fact.)

- So, was it Margaret the Martyr's death that inspired that boy from York to turn his military skills to plotting against his Protestant monarch?

Oh, a final fact for you: the boy's name was Guy Fawkes.

REASON TO REVOLT 3

PREJUDICE

'Prejudice is a great time saver. You can form opinions without having to get the facts.'

E. B. WHITE (1899–1985) – AMERICAN WRITER

Most people enjoy labels. They make life simpler, don't they? If history is anything to go by, there is a sense of security when you identify with people of a similar religion, football team or skin colour.

The problem is – and always will be – that as soon as you assume the uniform, someone will come along in a different colour. The result? Conflict. Hooligans. The purples cling to other purples in their purple-ness and any other colour is a potential enemy.

The sensible people (like you) seek out the similarities between us and not the differences. And at the end of the day, when all else fails – there is one common label we can stick on every person on the planet. That label says, 'We are all human.'

Sadly, too many people have ignored that label – or maybe they just can't read.

MASSACRE OF JEWS – BENEDICT OF YORK, 1190

The Norman lords enjoyed fighting. When they weren't murdering deer in their private forests they were fighting one another over minor quarrels. The Pope declared this was very naughty and they would never get into heaven if they killed a fellow Christian. The knights took off their helmets and scratched their heads and had a thought (just the one, shared between their brain cell). 'Hey, your holiness, would it be all right if we killed non-Christians then?'

And the Pope said (I'm paraphrasing), 'That's a great idea, you fellows. Kill those Muslims that are infesting our Holy Land and you'll earn a get-out-of-jail pardon for any Christians you've killed, as well as a free pass straight through the gates of heaven. No queuing.'

In 1095 Pope Urban II asked for knights to fight for the Christian Church in the Middle East, and so the crusades began. The Pope didn't mind the odd bit of exaggeration to stir up the pacifists. He claimed:

The Turks cut open the navels of Christians that they want
to torment with a loathsome death. They tear out their
organs and tie them to a stake. They drag their victims round
the stake and flog them. They kill them as they lie flat on the
ground with their entrails out. They tie some to posts and
shoot them full of arrows. They order others to bare their
necks and attack them with swords trying to see if they can
cut off their heads with a single stroke.

His statement wouldn't stand up to a fact-check; he was repeating rumours and inventions.

On the crusaders' march towards Jerusalem, they stopped to besiege the town of Ma'arrat. Once they had overrun the city walls, the hungry Christian soldiers realized they had captured a city with no food. Radulph of Caen recalled, 'Our troops boiled heathen adults in cooking pots, placed children on spits and ate them grilled.' Afterwards, the crusaders wrote to the Pope to apologize for this faux pas. They asked if he'd forgive them, for they'd only eaten chargrilled human when they were really hungry, and it's not as though they were eating Christians.

The cannibal crusaders climbed over the walls of Jerusalem on 15 June 1099 – three years after they had set off from Europe. As usual, they massacred the Turks inside. This time they had an extra reason for cutting up corpses. A lot of the Turks fought with their gold in their mouth so the crusaders couldn't get it. When they were cornered they swallowed the gold like a human piggy bank. It did them no good. The crusaders learnt about the trick and took the money out the shortest way – through the front.

Pope Urban's crusade had succeeded. News was sent back to Rome. With tragic timing his Holiness had hopped it to his heavenly home just two days before the news arrived.

The Turks fought back, which necessitated the Second Crusade to rescue the first lot. That crusade failed. In 1189 the Third Crusade began and the following year English warrior-king Richard the Lionheart would set off to join it. Richard was up against tough Turk Saladin and failed. But by this time, war-fever had taken over Europe and gripped the nation of England.

In September 1189, before he left, Richard was crowned. When the prominent moneylender Benedict of York attended the coronation in London, he found there was anger at the presence of Jews like him. Taxes had been raised to top up the war-fund Richard demanded, and false rumours started that the new king had ordered the massacre of Jews. On his way back to York, Benedict was attacked and killed.

The war against a distant enemy was fuelling a fear of foreigners. As fear turned to hatred, many English citizens declared they wanted to take the law into their own hands and destroy the enemies of Christianity – a sort of domestic crusade. There weren't any Muslims available to bash, so they picked on an old favourite of Christian societies – the Jews.

The French-speaking Jews were a target that were easy to identify. They were also a 'soft' target – the bully boys could hurt them without fear of being hurt themselves. An excuse? Well, the Jews were accused of the blood libel (the myth that Jews used the blood of Christian children in their rituals). Towns like Lynn, Stamford, Bury St Edmunds and Lincoln saw Jewish homes and businesses vandalized, looted and burnt as well as the families massacred. The authorities stood by and watched.

The worst of these atrocities happened in York in 1190, when a riot led to a massacre of Jews in the castle. The sheriff of York – the city's law enforcer – had left for the Third Crusade. A fire broke out in the city. This was a regular occurrence but in the 1190 conflagration some citizens took advantage of the chaos to break into the late Benedict's house in Coney Street. The place was looted and everyone inside murdered. Sensing the tide of feeling was rising against them, the entire Jewish community fled to Clifford's Tower in the city where they were surrounded by the mob. The message was 'Convert to Christianity or die'. Some chronicles say that fathers chose to kill their families before taking their own lives. Others died when the wooden tower was torched. Some, it was said, threw themselves on the mercy of the attackers but found there was no mercy; they were slaughtered.

Clearly prejudice played a part here, but this story would be at home in the 'Money' chapter too. For many of the mob, religion was just a mask to hide the real reason for the trouble: greed.

The York rioters were stirred into action by members of the local gentry called Richard Malebisse, William Percy, Marmeduke Darell and Philip de Fauconberg, who used the crusades as a pretext to flaunt their saintly Christian devotion and show loyalty to Richard the Lionheart. These men also saw the riots as an opportunity to wipe out the extensive debts they owed to Jewish moneylenders in the city. They had all borrowed heavily from Jewish moneylenders, and their surety was that they were in line for royal appointments. Those benefits did not materialize so they could not afford to repay their debts.

After the massacre their first action was to burn the records of their debts held in the Minster. This absolved them from repayment to the king, who would acquire the property and debts owed to the murdered Jews.

The consciences of the mob were clean because they had their Christian God on their side. No one was punished. The city was fined £66, paid by the leading fifty-nine families. That's less than fifty pence per Jewish life.

ST SCHOLASTICA DAY RIOT, OXFORD – TOWN V. GOWN, 1355

Hatred of the outsider isn't restricted to religion or even nationality. Sometimes you just dislike someone because they aren't a 'local'. When the 'incomers' behave badly and irritate you then you feel justified in your urge to slap them about a bit. And if you are short of a convincing excuse to administer a slap, you might try something slightly off the wall.

The St Scholastica Day riot erupted on 10 February 1355 in Oxford. An epic students *v.* town brawl followed an argument about a cup of wine. St Scholastica was the patron saint of education, and some see this as an apt day for a student riot (though what education the students were seeking in a boozer is debatable).

It all began at the Swindlestock Tavern in Oxford, a city that was at that time home to a reputable university. Two bolshy students (are there any other sort?), Walter de Springheuse and Roger de Chesterfield, were enjoying a few flagons of wine. Actually, they weren't enjoying them, because they complained to the landlord John de Croydon about the quality. You have to suspect that it wasn't the first sip of wine that prompted their disgruntlement. It may have been their third bottle. Or (if you are an apologist for bolshy students) you may suspect that the landlord of a town-centre pub could spot the symptoms of inebriation and substituted an inferior wine (a.k.a. paint stripper) in the belief that the drinkers were too far gone to notice.*

---

* There are more synonyms for 'drunk' in the English language than almost any other word. In 2024 someone with a lot of patience

The tavern was populated that day by two factions who grated on one another at the best of times: the students and the towns-folk. The locals probably sided with the landlord – one of their own – and the students with Walter de Springheuse and Roger de Chesterfield – two of *their* own. Verbals turned to physicals when de Chesterfield emptied his wooden cup in the face of de Croydon then used the cup to smash him on the head. Today's thugs in pub or club might administer a 'glassing'. We must assume de Chesterfield gave de Croydon a good wooding. Blows were exchanged. Nobody died. (Yet.)

The locals were not noted for their tolerance. Just a hundred years or so before, in 1222, there is a recorded Oxford burning for heresy. A deacon of the Church was burnt at Oxford for embra-cing the Jewish faith so he could marry a Jew. It is the earliest recorded execution by burning and indicates the mindset of 'The Town'.

And there was a history of town *v.* gown violence amid the dreaming spires before the 1355 eruption. In 1209 an Oxford woman died and two of Oxford's pupils were lynched by citi-zens. (This resulted in another little band of victimized scholars scurrying off to Cambridge to set up a new university. There is no record of what Cambridge had done to deserve this.) Violence was often on a tit-for-tat basis – an Oxford student's murder

---

(and too much time on their hands) calculated there are 546 different words for 'drunk'. There are the formal: under the influence, intoxicated, inebriated; the informal: tipsy, plastered, hammered, sloshed, wasted, paralytic; and the slang: fried, looped, stewed, blitzed, zonked, smashed, three sheets to the wind.

of a citizen in 1298 was avenged by the townsfolk's murder of a student. An eye for an eye. The killers of the student were excommunicated and the town fined, whereas the academic assassin of the Oxford citizen went unpunished. This was the sort of inequity that kept the pressure cooker of resentment bubbling.

To add to the violence, students often rioted among themselves, with a 1314 riot breaking out between northern students and those from the south. Murder and manslaughter ensued but the thirty-nine perpetrators were either granted church sanctuary or escaped punishment. The locals would not have been treated so leniently.

When the 1355 Swindlestock Tavern brawl spilt out into the streets, both sides summoned reinforcements using church bells. The chancellor of the university arrived to mediate and was greeted with a shower of arrows. As the chancellor pleaded for peace and good will, the town bailiffs were urging the people of Oxford to arm themselves in self-defence. (It is invariably 'self-defence', isn't it?) Agricultural labourers came in from the surrounding farms with their pitchforks and scythes to join in the sport. They didn't even lose out on their wages, because the bailiffs were paying them as yeomanry peacekeepers.

The next day the halls of residence were invaded and, after the townsfolk had snaffled the food there, they turned on the cowering students and maimed or murdered them. Some of the more dramatic (or fanciful) chronicles said that clerics associated with the university were scalped. 'Fanciful' because it's difficult to scalp someone with a scythe and impossible with a pitchfork. Student corpses were thrown into the Thames or dumped in toilet pits and dunghills.

Students fled, outnumbered and out-scythed. Without fuel a bonfire dies and, with no students left to assault, the rage of the Oxford people abated. At the end of the riots the score was thirty townies dead and around fifty gownies.

King Edward III did little to dampen the fires of local resentment. He not only pardoned the students but fined the town and imprisoned the mayor and bailiffs. He then issued a royal charter to emphasize that student rights exceeded those of the town. A royal stitch-up that would ensure the locals would bear a grudge against the student incomers in perpetuity. The chancellor (who'd escaped the arrows) was given the right to raise taxes on bread and drink in the town. Future town *v.* gown disputes (perish the thought) would be adjudicated on by the university.

Down the centuries the balance of power has been restored. The students now expend their energies on protesting international issues, pulling down statues, drinking and occasionally attending a lecture . . . all at the expense of the British taxpayers. The locals continue to mutter darkly into their wooden cups of wine as they count the dollars, yen and euros that the foreign students bring to their wooden coffers. Incomer equals income.

Prejudice or tolerance. Love or hate. It's all a matter of degrees.

LESSONS FROM HISTORY 3

CHOOSE YOUR WEAPON

'The tree of liberty must be refreshed from time to time with the blood of patriots and tyrants. It is its natural manure.'

THOMAS JEFFERSON (1743–1826) – THIRD US PRESIDENT

Rebellions are the mothers of invention – often the invention of better weapons. Conflicts can breed arms races. They can also breed innovation, where opponents make use of whatever comes to hand.

TILE

King Pyrrhus of Epirus (319–272 BC) had fought and survived bitter battles against tough enemies such as Rome.* But it was a rebellion that led to his demise – not

---

* Although he technically won his first two battles against Rome, he lost so many good men that it didn't feel like he'd won at all. This hollow kind of success became known as a 'Pyrrhic victory'.

much more than a street fight. In 272 BC he intervened in Argos, Greece, where one of the in-fighting factions asked him to restore order. Argos proved a catalogue of errors for the conquering king.

Pyrrhus rode in to engage in street fighting even though the revolt wasn't really any of his business. A peasant foot soldier prodded the king with a pike. Pyrrhus turned on him with his sword. Unfortunately, the peasant's mother was watching over her son from the roof of their house. You can imagine her cries of, 'Leave my lovely boy alone, you brute,' as she seized the only weapon to hand: a tile from her roof. With the skill of an Olympic discus thrower, she skimmed it at the king and caught his neck, just below the back of his helmet. He fell from his horse, stunned, and was decapitated by the rebels. An embarrassing and ignominious end for any renowned warrior.

HELLBURNERS

When the Spanish Armada arrived in 1588, its huge ships were defeated with hellburner ships – floating firebombs sent into their midst. The idea had first been used four years earlier in the Eighty Years' War (1568–1648) between the Spanish and the Dutch. The Protestant Dutch rebelled against the Catholic Spanish in 1568, and the hub of their resistance was Antwerp. By July 1584, Antwerp was isolated and vulnerable and under siege from the Spanish navy that had built a ship-bridge across the river

Scheldt to cut off supplies to the defenders. The Dutch were starving, with even supplies of Edam running out. That ship-bridge had to be destroyed or, as the Dutch might say, un-clogged. They had help. Elizabeth I of England provided money to her fellow Protestants and Federigo Giambelli was the engineer with the idea for the hellburners. They were early weapons of mass destruction.

Two merchant ships, *Fortune* and *Hope*, would be packed with gunpowder and floated into the ship-bridge. The clever part was the fuse, which would be triggered by a clockwork and flintlock mechanism. A time bomb. Old ploughs and stone slabs laid over the powder chamber would add shrapnel to the damage. Where would they get these slabs? They used tombstones, assuming the dead Dutch would be happy to contribute to keeping their relatives alive.

Thirty-two normal fireships were dispatched to deceive the Spanish. Last came the hellburners. Their decks were stacked with little bonfires to make them look like conventional fireships. Brave pilots had held on to the Dutch helms (no pun intended). At the last moment they escaped in a skiff, grateful that the timer hadn't gone off early. Clearly that took Dutch courage.

Fortune had the bad fortune to run aground some way short of the target. The Spanish troops saw the decoy fire fizzle out. Oh, how they laughed. But *Hope* achieved its goal. When it ran into the bridge, Spanish soldiers climbed aboard to extinguish the puny little decoy fires on the deck, unaware they were standing on a tomb-bomb.

The explosion killed eight hundred Spanish troops. The destruction was immense as debris rained down, mixed with Spanish heads and limbs. The relief of Antwerp was not successful, but the rebel invention changed the course of history . . . and gave Elizabeth I a payoff for her investment.

The Spanish Armada arrived to conquer the Tudor queen's kingdom four years later. Their ships anchored near the shores of the Spanish Netherlands and the small port of Gravelines. From there, they planned to escort the troop barges across the Channel to invade England. As they lay at anchor on the night of 7/8 August, the English sent fireships into their midst. Five of them got through. These were filled with tar but very little gunpowder since the English ships were running short. The psychological effect was enormous. After their experience at Antwerp, the Spanish thought the English were employing hellburners and panicked. They cut their anchors and, breaking formation, the Spanish flew (how do these unintended puns keep slipping in?). The runaways fatally weakened the Armada's battle-line.

There were no exploding gravestones at Gravelines. There didn't have to be. The fear of them was enough.

Storms finished off the attempted invasion. Commemorative medals were struck, wisely giving credit to God for sending the storms. The inscription read, 'God blew, and they were scattered.' Elizabeth became revered as the woman who defeated the Armada; she did, but her investment in hellburners during the Antwerp siege is often forgotten.

GOLD

In 1599 the Jivaro tribes of Ecuador became annoyed at the way the Spanish governor was taxing them. He demanded higher quotas of gold from their mines and inflicted that old favourite irritant, a poll tax (essentially a tax on being alive). The Jivaro were hunters, farmers and warriors and the oppression boiled over into revolt. Literally boiled over. The warriors captured the greedy governor and from the myriad methods of execution they selected a darkly ironic one: they poured molten gold down his throat. The glittering end to a less-than-glittering career. Thermal injury to the lungs would cause instant death while the steam pressure generated in the digestive system would probably cause the bowels to explode. That would be fun to watch.

CHEESE

If you don't have a weapon to hand, you'll have to improvise.

In 1766, the people of Nottingham were hungry because merchants from wealthier areas of the country were buying Nottingham foods at inflated prices that the locals couldn't afford. Some merchants from Lincolnshire bought a large consignment of Nottingham cheese to sell on in their home county, and that was the last cheese straw. The Lincoln dealers were accosted by a gang of 'rude lads' who demanded they share the cheese. Violence erupted and the targets were the cheese shops, which had their windows broken and their cheeses looted.

The mayor of Nottingham was the man to put a halt to this rebellious behaviour. He took to the streets and courageously faced the rebel mob. They were unarmed (unless they had brought a cheese grater, which is generally considered ineffective against a solid mayoral chain). Imagine the mayor's horror when the crowd parted, and the rioters revealed their secret weapon. A 50-kilo wheel of cheese.

Being a wheel, it rolled inexorably towards him down the slope of the street called (of course) Wheeler Gate. He just wasn't nimble enough to dodge the collision and, before you could say Wensleydale, he was knocked flat. The mob had humiliated the big cheese of Nottingham.

When the troops finally arrived, an unfortunate farmer called William Eggleston was standing on guard beside the cheeses he'd brought to market. They mistook him for a looter and shot him dead. The rioting went on for several days until the cheese wagons of the foreign merchants were arranged into a convoy and escorted by the militia. Very Caerphilly.

GUILLOTINE

People have recovered from hanging. Very few, it's true. But apart from being just 99 per cent effective it has also seen a lot of people die slowly and painfully from strangulation.

Separating the head from a body, however, you'll find is a much more efficient method.

Dr Joseph-Ignace Guillotin proposed this more humane method of execution in France during the Revolution. It is usually forgotten that the doctor himself was opposed to capital punishment. But with a Gallic sigh and shrug he told the National Assembly that if executions must happen, they should be swift and painless.

Guillotin did not invent the guillotine, he merely proposed it. Decapitation 'by means of a simple mechanism' would be just the ticket. And so, the *louisette* was developed by the king's doctor, Antoine Louis. The chief executioner, Charles-Henri Sanson, later suggested that it was King Louis XVI himself who proposed the efficient angled blade that distinguished the machine from cruder mechanisms going back to Roman times. If so, then King Louis's opinion regarding the effectiveness of the blade on his own neck is not recorded. Nor did the other 17,000 victims of the device care to comment.

Dr Guillotin received no royalties for his consideration even though the machine proved a massive crowd-pleaser. Within days of his proposal being accepted, a comic song was written about 'his' machine. During the Reign of Terror, programme sellers even cashed in with lists of the condemned at that day's butchery. Madame Tussaud originally made her name by modelling death masks of the beheaded heads of the aristocrats – her former friends. All the show lacked was confectioners selling candy-lolly heads on sticks to the kids.

In 1795, a newspaper published the view that a victim's head remained conscious for several minutes after death and that disturbed Dr Guillotin enormously. He went to his grave (head attached) regretting that the death-dealing device carried his name. Despite this, Guillotin is wrongly remembered by many as the man who invented the 'National Razor'.

MACHINE GUN

A Victorian wit boasted that the British Empire ruled the world courtesy of the machine gun.

> Whatever happens
> We have got
> The Maxim gun . . .
> And they have not.
>
> HILAIRE BELLOC, 'THE MODERN TRAVELLER', 1898

Smug that may be. But it is largely true. Of course, when the machine gun was met with other machine guns, the world ended up with the stalemate of the trenches on the Western Front in the First World War.

Big official armies have always had access to the best kit, with state-backed arsenals and weapon-smiths. As early as the fourth century BC, the Greeks had invented the *cheiroballista*, a large machine device powered by twisted rope torsion. It could launch either large stones or a hail of smaller projectiles, creating a devastating volley of fire on enemy formations. Rebels, on the other hand, often had to improvise, but they could still be inventive and potentially deadly.

In 1835 the Italian revolutionary Giuseppe Fiesci created the homemade 'Infernal Machine'. His target was King Louis-Philippe of France on his way to inspect his troops. Fiesci rigged up a machine to fire twenty-five guns all at once. He mounted rifle barrels on a wooden frame and loaded each barrel with around eight bullets and twenty lead pellets. A trail of gunpowder meant a single fuse could fire the twenty-five barrels simultaneously.

After the assassination attempt, French artillery officers said that if Fiesci had had some artillery knowledge, his Infernal Machine could have been devastating, killed two hundred people and torn King Louis to tatters. It could. But what did happen?

Fiesci pointed the barrels out of a window facing the boulevard that Louis would drive down. The fuse was lit, the guns discharged, but the assassin failed. Louis survived with a scratch on his forehead. Unfortunately, eighteen innocent people died and another twenty-two were injured, of whom four had to undergo amputations. (Louis's horse would also die later from its wounds, but it isn't generally included in the casualties.) In a form of instant karma, Fiesci received wounds to his head, hands and face from the explosions. It did not prevent his escape, but the trail of blood led to his being traced and arrested.

Fiesci was sent to the guillotine which, unlike his Infernal Machine, had a 100 per cent success rate.

It's fair to say neither tiles nor cheese ever caught on as a weapon of choice. But some of these arms races have benefits we enjoy today. Aeroplanes in 1914 were little better than the Wright Brothers' kites of wood and canvas that first flew in 1903. Then the First World War forces' need for 'air superiority' meant that just four years after hostilities began, the range and altitude of planes had doubled while speeds increased by 50 per cent.

Modern computers? Developed by the need to improve the accuracy of artillery shells during the Second World War and now used by trolls to direct verbal venom at victims.

The Third World War will certainly accelerate the effectiveness of nuclear bunkers . . . but only for the politicians and aristocrats who will build them using your taxes. You won't revolt against that little injustice because you'll be vaporized. (Unless you offer to become one of the loyal royal servants. They will be needed to polish the radioactive fallout dust from their employers' shoes.)

'Twas ever thus.

REASON TO REVOLT 4
SLAVERY

'If slavery is not wrong, nothing is wrong.'
ABRAHAM LINCOLN (BEFORE HE WAS ASSASSINATED
BY A PRO-SLAVER)

If you have been enslaved then you may be resigned to your
fate. Your will to break free could be sapped and your body
too undernourished and weak for a struggle against your owners.
Some of your tormentors build castles, churches or stately homes
and palaces to remind you of their power, statements in stone
that say, 'Look on my Works, ye would-be rebels, and despair.'
Worse, they probably used your muscle power to build those palaces, not to mention the prisons that will keep you in your place.
But perhaps you lie on your pallet of straw, sucking on your daily
crust, and fall asleep to dream of the day when you will throw off
the chains and wrap them round the throats of your tyrannical
owners.

Today's wage-slaves have their metaphorical chains. Not the
physical deprivations of the serfs, but the mental whips of the
alarm clock, the treadmill of routine and the helplessness against

the tyranny of the bosses. (Yes, I too worked for the North East-ern Electricity Board in the 1960s.) But it's easy for our whingeing wage-slaves of the twenty-first century to forget how much worse the whips and treadmills of real slavery were (and still are for millions of unfortunates). We forget how perilous past protests have been, be they in the dark satanic mills of industry or the cotton fields of America.

In 1843 the feminist and social activist Flora Tristan wrote, 'Workers of the world, unite. You have nothing to lose but your chains.' This rallying cry was copied five years later by revolu-tionary theorist Karl Marx (1818–83). By then Flora had died at the age of forty-one, so she didn't sue him for plagiarism. Marx liked the sentiment so much he had 'Workers of all lands, unite' inscribed on his gravestone. You'll notice he dropped the last part. The phrase 'you have nothing to lose' is a little optimistic. You have everything to lose if you fail to throw off your chains. Karl himself was a stirrer, not an activist; there is no evidence that he ever personally participated in any revolutionary acts. He kept his bowels inside his belly and his neck free of rope.

Would you strive to lose your chains if the odds were on you losing your head, your eyes, your limbs, or your life? Would you cry, 'Give me liberty or give me death'? (A beautifully balanced sentence, as eloquent as it is stupid.) It's 'give me death' that's the thorny bit, isn't it? The quote was allegedly said by the American revolutionary Patrick Henry (1736–99) as he urged his fellow Brits in America to free themselves from their Brits-in-Britain rulers. Paddy Henry would know all about 'liberty': he bought and sold slaves who worked his land. Liberty? A fine sentiment, Mr Henry.

You probably think you have a good chance of liberty when you set off down the revolting road. Some examples may help you calculate your chances. To assess the odds against a successful revolt, let's look back into the slave rebellions of the past. Toss the coin. Heads you win; tails and you lose your head. The coin is spinning.

SPARTACUS AND THE SERVILE WARS

One of the most famous slave revolts in history was against the Roman Republic. Ancient Rome is often called a 'civilization', but there wasn't much that was civilized about their economy, which relied on slave labour. As for their 'games', they relied on the slaughter of humans and animals for entertainment. The blood-soaked sands of the arenas don't so much cast a shadow over the glory of Rome as a total eclipse.

The best-remembered slave revolt was the one led by Spartacus. But Spartacus didn't invent the Roman slave uprising. His efforts were actually part of the Third Servile War (the word 'servile' being derived from *servus*, Latin for 'slave'). Spartacus was inspired by the first two Servile Wars, yet he didn't seem to take on board the fact that they failed in the end. Or maybe Spartacus thought he had nothing to lose but his chains.

The First Servile War broke out in Sicily and lasted three years (135–132 BC). It was led by the Syrian slave Eunus, a fire-breather and a conjuror who claimed to be a prophet who heard voices telling him he would one day be a king. If he'd been a half-decent prophet then he'd have prophesied the unhappy end to his adventures.

Sicily was a fertile land, and Roman aristocrats had bought large tracts to farm this 'breadbasket of the Roman Republic'. They relied, naturally, on slave labour from prisoners of war, or human captives bought from entrepreneurial pirates or from the slave markets of North Africa. Roman conquests kept creating more provinces, and the governors of the subjugated people found a fun way to make a quick denarius: they organized 'hunts' to capture the indigenous people and sell them to landowners in places like Sicily as cheap labour. The market was soon flooded, and prices fell. Sicilian landowners found that slaves were so cheap it was more economical to wear out the workers and replace them than pay to feed and accommodate them humanely.*

The Greek historian Diodorus Siculus described the lives of the Sicilian slaves: 'They were treated like animals, as they were driven in droves like so many herds of cattle from the different places where they were bred and brought up . . . they were branded with certain marks burnt on their bodies.' They had no days off and worked the fields in chains. The enslavers kept them hungry and badly clothed. The slaves spent their few sleeping hours in hot, underground dormitories. The European Court of Human Rights had clearly not been invented.

Refusing to tolerate this treatment any longer, in 135 BC Eunus led a force of four hundred slaves into Enna city, where they killed the masters and their families. With a curious nod to 'justice', the slaves set up courts to try their Roman victims. Those

---

* A couple of millennia later, in 1955, the magazine *Life* published an article bemoaning 'throwaway living' and the term 'throwaway society' was born, but as ever, the Romans got there first.

found 'guilty' – probably around 100 per cent – were tortured and executed. Maybe it was partly an attempt to show their righteousness, but those 'trials' definitely allowed the slaves to prolong the misery of their erstwhile masters. It was the same as the Romans enjoying victims being torn apart in the arenas when a quick, clean chop would have had the same end result. We know that one of the city's ruthless slave owners, Damophilus, was dragged through the streets to the theatre where he was butchered in a true Roman 'games' style. His wife was tortured to death by her own servants. How sweet a revenge must that have been.

The slaves spared the blacksmiths and chained them to their forges while they made weapons for the growing rebel army. Damophilus's daughter was renowned among the poor for trying to alleviate slave suffering, so she was given safe passage to a Roman garrison. Even today that would be seen as a humanitarian gesture on the part of a rebel army. As the rebellion grew, another leader, Cleon, added fighters to Eunus's slave forces. Women and children swelled the rebel forces to more than seventy thousand. They defeated everything the Roman senate could throw at them. Embarrassing.

After two years of defeats, Rome sent in an army commanded by soldier and statesman Publius Rupilius. Ruthless Rupilius besieged the major slave fortress of Tauromenium and left the inhabitants so hungry they resorted to eating their horses and then turned to cannibalism. The original serf and turf perhaps. A treacherous (and obviously very hungry) slave opened the gates and let in the Roman enemy. The rebel fighters in Tauromenium were first tortured and then thrown off a cliff. Rupilius's Roman legions then marched on to Cleon's capital of Enna. Cleon sallied out to fight or die trying. He died trying. Rupilius showed the body of Cleon to the defenders on the walls, and they gave up.

Now, as an upper-class Roman, you'd have to be aware that a united slave rebellion was a massive danger. So, you'd want to discourage each individual slave from seeing an uprising and trying one of their own. You'd bring in an especially vicious punishment for slaves. A very public and visual deterrent. This time the punishment was crucifixion, for all twenty thousand.

The Romans seem to have preferred nails, large iron ones, which were expensive at the time. After death those green- (or mean-)minded Romans could recycle them for the next crucifixion. The nails were probably driven through the hand into the carpal tunnel or between the two main forearm bones, the ulna and radius. This would give a good firm fix to the wood and also go through (or rub against) the radial nerve, increasing the amount of pain. At the foot end, nails would either go through the heel bone individually into wood or, with the feet crossed, a nail would be driven through the ankles, equivalent to the wrist position of the nails.

This would cause blood loss both before and after the cross was raised and contribute to death from exsanguination. Once the cross was vertical, the victim's chest would be painfully compressed, and breathing would be harder.* The executioners could also add a small block of wood under the feet, so you suffered for longer. Death was usually from a combination of infection

---

* This death was particularly slow and painful which gave us the term excruciating, from the Latin meaning 'from crucifying'.

(wounds getting dirty from nails, flogging etc.), hypovolaemia (blood loss, dehydration), heart arrythmia, heart failure and sometimes pulmonary emboli from clots (since the victims were both immobile and dehydrated). The time taken to die would range from a few hours to days. It initially depended on the strength of the person; the amount of blood loss from flogging would determine how fast they dehydrated under the heat of the sun, as would whether their 'friends' provided drinks to keep them hydrated. Real friends broke the legs of the suffering, to stop them supporting the upper body and put the victim out of their misery quicker.

For the 'civilized' Romans, crucifixion is a bloody shame. That is the reality. But we might question the historical reporting of this Servile War. Consider twenty thousand crucifixions. That's an awful lot of work for a small army of carpenters, nailmakers, hole-diggers and executioners. A small forest would be destroyed. It would certainly suit the Romans to exaggerate for effect. Likewise, reports of cannibalism among the rebels come from a Roman source, and Latin chronicles liked to make the enemies of Rome appear more barbaric than they really were.

Whatever the true numbers, the crucifixions were a clear message to the remaining slaves under 'King' Eunus. He fled to the Sicilian hills with a small force who beheaded one another rather than face a slow Roman death. Eunus was found hiding in a cave (head still attached). He was imprisoned but cheated the Roman plans to make an example of him by public execution. He died of an illness. Compared to crucifixion this was a smart move. Dead clever.

The Roman brutality shown to the defeated was a reminder to slaves everywhere to know their place. But it was a message writ in water because a Second Servile War followed around thirty years later in 104 BC. The enslaved of Sicily ought to have learnt from the First Servile War but clearly didn't.

Six hundred Roman soldiers were sent to quell this second servile uprising in the mountains of the island. They were beaten and butchered, except for the sensible ones who threw away their weapons and ran. The rebels grew in confidence, as you would. A similar pattern followed.

A slave leader called Salvius emerged and called himself 'The Slave King'. He claimed to be descended from Syrian royalty and there was no Wikipedia to prove him a liar. Salvius was modelling himself on Eunus from the First Servile War. Like Eunus he was famed for being a prophet and his swelling army captured unprepared cities.

A further large rebellion of ten thousand slaves broke out in the west, led by Athenion who was well known as (stop me if you've heard this one) a prophet. The two slave leaders joined forces. The senate back in Rome resorted to their secret weapon, alliteration, and appointed the legendary Lucius Licinius Lucullus to lead the legions.

Slave King Salvius retreated to a fortified city where he was joined by his pal Athenion. Salvius died of unknown causes. (Yet again, the prophet hadn't seen that coming.) Athenion took control and now faced Gaius Marius – Rome's top general. In a scene that could have been invented for a Hollywood movie, Gaius Marius came face to face with Athenion in one-to-one combat. The Roman was wounded but fought back to kill the slave leader. The slave army dissolved.

A thousand of the captured slaves came up with a new way

to defy their enslavers. They were offered the chance to go to Rome to fight wild animals for the entertainment of the populace. The slaves declined and cheated the baying, paying public by killing one another. The last man standing fell on his own sword, which is quicker than crucifixion but just as fatal. The second rebellion had failed – but the aura of Roman invincibility was dented.

After another gap of around thirty years the Third Servile War broke out in 73 BC, and this was the most serious because the City of Rome itself came under threat. It began with an escape of around seventy enslaved gladiators. They were led by a Thracian (from modern-day Bulgaria) and his name was Spartacus. He was an ex-Roman soldier, so you'd expect him to have more military nous than the Sicilian swineherds and domestics. That said, one theory is that his breakout wasn't aimed so much at overthrowing the Roman Empire as simply going home to his own people. He missed his mum.

The rebels rampaged through Italy gathering supporters while the legions were occupied elsewhere. So far so easy. They camped on Mount Vesuvius as a defensible position and were surrounded by the Romans who hoped to starve them into submission. Spartacus's military mind outwitted them. His men used ropes – ingeniously made from vines – to scale down the inside walls of the volcano and attack their enemy from behind. Success in a rebellion is a magnet that draws the timid to the cause and in two years there was a formidable army of seventy thousand ranged against Rome.

The Roman senate asked for a volunteer to lead the response and only Crassus responded. He had forty thousand under his command and discipline was harsh. Crassus drove the rebels south and Spartacus decided to cross to that old centre of Servile Wars one and two, Sicily.

The military skills of Spartacus may have been exemplary, but his people skills were wanting. He paid pirates to transport his army across to the island. A pirate is just a robber with waterwings. They took Spartacus's money and abandoned him. What did he expect?

The rebels were soundly defeated soon after, because their organization collapsed in the heat of battle. Spartacus probably died in that last scrap. Romantics may prefer to believe that he slipped away and finally made it back home to Thrace and Mum's cooking.

Two thousand years later, the Spartacus story was made into a movie. The screenwriter wrote in a fictional scene where the defeated rebel survivors are asked to point out which of their number is Spartacus and are threatened with torture. They refuse to identify their leader (dead or alive) to protect the man. You'd not do that, would you? If a torturer politely asked me to identify Spartacus, I'd say, 'It's that bloke over there that looks a lot like Kirk Douglas.' But in a Hollywood display of heroic unity, the defeated start crying out, 'I am Spartacus,' so they all shared the same fate.

The 'I am Spartacus' moment never happened, but six thousand were crucified – maybe including Spartacus. That's another forest ruined. Slave revolts may have right on their side, and some have might. But the Romans had the magic ingredient: discipline.

Sadly, throughout history, slave revolts almost always fail.

Almost. There was one successful slave uprising in history that ended in a free, independent nation.

TOUSSAINT LOUVERTURE AND THE HAITIAN SLAVE REVOLT, 1791

American rebel Benjamin Franklin (1706–90) once said, 'Rebellion against tyrants is obedience to God.'

Franklin – the American political thinker – had to say that, of course, because he was one of the leaders of the American Revolution in its rebellion against the British 'tyrants'. This 'tyranny' involved passing laws and raising taxes in the UK without the American Brits in the colonies having any say in it. The colonists had no MPs to argue their case in Parliament. But Mr Franklin's 'obedience to God' would not extend to women. It would be almost 150 years before they had that freedom to vote against tyrants. And when Franklin made that endorsement of rebellion he wasn't thinking of Joseph, Bob, Peter, Othello, King, George or Jemima – his slaves. And it would be interesting to know what Mr Franklin would have made of the Haitian slave revolt, which began a year after he died.

Christopher Columbus was the first European to land on Haiti, in 1492. Chris always believed he had landed in India and that's why he called the natives 'Indians'. It was the start of hundreds of years of misery for the indigenous people of the island.

In 1495, the Spanish rounded up five hundred Arawak Indians on Haiti and sent them to Spain. They took another five hundred to work for them on the islands. Half the slaves transported to Spain died on the Atlantic crossing, but callous Columbus shrugged and wrote home: 'Though they die now they will not always die. We can send all the slaves from here that you can sell.' He turned out to be as wrong about that 'not always die' claim as he was about the Americas being India.

The Arawaks were made to grow food, dig for gold or spin cotton for their conquerors. Any Indian who declined the offer of employment would have their nose or ears lopped off, and be sent back to the village as a warning to the others. Each worker over the age of fourteen was given a quota of ore to be mined. At the end of a successful month, they'd be given a copper token to wear around their neck. Any man or woman caught without a token would face a punishment – in the most severe cases, they would have a hand cut off. The Arawaks spent so much time earning their tokens they hadn't time to feed their families.

The Indians couldn't rebel against the superior weaponry of the Spanish occupiers. Many killed themselves – by hanging, by poison or by throwing themselves onto sharpened wood stakes. Sometimes a hundred at a time jumped off a cliff. Many mothers killed their children to save them from a life of misery.

A few Arawaks tried to fight back in 1495 and Columbus's son, Ferdinand, wrote about a savage tactic used against the Indians. 'The most terrible weapons were the twenty attack dogs who immediately tore the Indians apart. These animals ripped open the limbs and bellies and chased fleeing Indians into the bush.' Any Indians captured alive were simply killed. In later years, these dogs were used to hunt Indians just for sport as the Spanish regressed to the cruelties of the Roman arenas. Spanish history writer Bartolomé de las Casas wrote, 'The Spaniards still do nothing save tear the natives to shreds, murder them and

inflict upon them untold misery, suffering and distress, torment-
ing, harrying and persecuting them mercilessly.'

Forced work and European diseases killed all of the Arawaks
off in time, but not revolution in Haiti. For those Arawak and
other local slave workers were replaced by the import of more
than 10 million African slaves in the terrible transatlantic trade
over the next three hundred years.

In 1791 the French Revolution inspired the slaves in the French
colony of Haiti to bid for freedom on the principle, 'What's good
enough for Paris is good enough for Port-au-Prince.' The slaves
in the north of the island slaughtered around two thousand of
their French and British masters. The rebel leaders that were
captured by the French were 'broken on the wheel' – an agonizing form of mutilation with echoes of crucifixion.

'Breaking on the wheel', also known as the 'Catherine wheel',
involved:

- Tying the condemned to a large breaking wheel before
  crushing the limbs and bones . . . sometimes over several
  days, working upwards from the ankles.
- Weaving the broken body through the spokes before hoisting
  it on a pole so the crowds could witness it.
- Sometimes the victim was put out of his misery, but some
  survived for many hours. A fire might be lit under the wheel
  to add to the spectacle and the suffering.

At your next firework display, you may like to remember the historical meaning behind the fizzing Catherine wheel.

This sort of retribution did not endear the masters to the slaves. Toussaint Louverture (1743–1803) was a former slave who turned an undisciplined slave revolt into a revolutionary campaign. Ironically, he had become rich enough to buy coffee plantations and own slaves himself. He didn't argue for the abolition of slavery in the first instance, just an extra day of rest for the enslaved people and a ban on the whip as punishment. The French governor refused. Toussaint hardened his resolve, demanding the complete abolition of slavery in Haiti.

Toussaint proved to be an astute leader of the rebels and used cunning alliances with the British and Spanish enemies of France to ensure victory. Then, when the French backed the abolition of slavery, Toussaint switched sides to fight for France against the British and Spanish. Some might call him an opportunist. He was certainly an egoist, but these are the things that often make a successful leader.

He used his success to persuade the French to make him governor-general, abolished slavery and kept the economy strong by giving wages to freed slaves to carry on the plantation work.

In 1801 Toussaint helped create a new constitution that made him governor-general for life (nobody's perfect) and Haiti a free French colony. Toussaint's constitution stated: 'There cannot exist slaves in Haiti, servitude is therein forever abolished. All men are born, live and die free and French.'

The enslaved may have been free but the state of Haiti wasn't 'free' yet. For Napoleon ruled France and he didn't like Toussaint declaring a constitution without consulting him. Napoleon was not a man to cross. In 1802 he sent a French army to Haiti under Charles Leclerc with secret orders to arrest Toussaint. The

Haitian governor was shipped back to France, shut in a dungeon, and died of cold and hunger within a year.

He didn't live to see his campaign for independence succeed, but his lieutenant carried on the fight against the French dictator's army. Two-thirds of Leclerc's force died. In 1803 the French gave up trying to crush the former slaves of Haiti. By this time, 400,000 people of Haiti and Europe had died in the struggles. Haiti won its independence in 1804, just as Toussaint Louverture had striven for.

What finished the French? Yellow fever. It even killed Leclerc (which served him right).

Toussaint Louverture has been called 'The Black Spartacus', which is fanciful. Apart from anything else, his rebellion actually succeeded. But sometimes historians like to patronize us by using shorthand like that. Toussaint Louverture was Toussaint Louverture. As unique as you.

WILLIAM WILBERFORCE AND THE ABOLITION OF SLAVERY, 1787

Britain didn't invent slavery but it certainly profited from the trade in human misery. It was one of the first nations to lead a campaign to abolish the slave trade, though cynics have suggested that the humanitarian movement didn't gain traction till after the slave trade became unprofitable.

The change, when it came, was not the result of rioting or rebellion. It was done through legal channels and the other 'R' word: 'Reform'. But it was revolutionary nonetheless.

In the simplistic world of history education there is usually a standout name for students to cling to like a buoy in a swirling sea. Prison reform? Elizabeth Fry. Votes for Women? Emmeline Pankhurst. American oppression of the Native Americans? General Custer. Abolition of slavery? That would be William Wilberforce (1759–1833).

The British MP campaigned tirelessly to keep the issue in the public spotlight, saying, 'You may choose to look the other way, but you can never say again that you did not know.'

So, did Wilberforce lead the abolitionist cause? History, like life, is never that simple. In 1787 in Britain there was a growing unease about slavery among the moralizing communities like the churches. The Church of England was on its slavery high horse. This was odd since its missionary arm had investments in a West Indies slave colony, where the slaves were branded on the chest with the word 'Society'. Apparently someone had decided it would be cruel to brand people with the full name: 'The Society for the Propagation of the Gospel in Foreign Parts'.

Public aversion to the slave trade was heightened by incidents like the *Zong* massacre of 1781. This British slave ship had been delayed in its Atlantic crossing – maybe a navigational error – and the crew was running short of drinking water in the heat of the Caribbean. Their solution was to take the less valuable slaves and throw them overboard.

Contemporary reports of the *Zong* massacre make grim reading. On 29 November, the crew assembled and unanimously agreed that jettisoning of slaves would be a sound tactic.

- That day, fifty-four women and children were thrown through cabin windows.

- Two days later forty-two men were thrown overboard and thirty-six were to follow.
- A further ten Africans, in a display of defiance, jumped into the sea.
- Hearing the cries of the victims led one of the captives to request that the others be starved rather than drowned. The crew declined.
- 142 Africans were killed by the time the ship reached Jamaica.

The atrocity might have passed unnoticed by the British public, but the ship owners had the effrontery to *claim on their insurance* for the lost income the slave sales would have earned: £30 per slave to be exact. The insurance company declined to pay – maybe the small print said the massacre of your assets was excluded from the third-party, fire and theft clause.

The ship owners had invoked the 'general average' rule, whereby a captain who jettisons part of his cargo to save the rest can claim for the loss from his insurers. The judge, Lord Mansfield, was keen to uphold the principle of the 'general average'. If your cargo of horses was taking on water then by all means, throw half the horses overboard to rescue an 'average' amount and claim the loss from your insurers. Mansfield's judgment stated: 'The case of slaves was the same as if horses had been thrown overboard.'

A slave = a horse? Really? As Mansfield gave his judgment was he humming the popular song from forty years before, 'Rule Britannia, Britannia rule the graves'?

And so the law books stated it plainly: humans had become commodities. The irony is that this incident was slap-bang in the middle of what overblown chroniclers have called 'The Age of Enlightenment' when (allegedly) thinkers in Europe fastened on the idea that humankind could be advanced through rational change. If the Enlightenment means throwing 130 people into the sea to drown, then bring back the Dark Ages.

Just as ironically, it was only five years since the USA had made its self-congratulatory 'Declaration of Independence' . . .

> We hold these truths to be self-evident, that all men are
> created equal, that they are endowed by their Creator with
> certain unalienable Rights, that among these are Life, Liberty
> and the pursuit of Happiness.

They forgot to add, 'So long as you are a Caucasian male.' How absent-minded of them.

Meanwhile, in Britain, the anti-slavery campaigner Granville Sharp worked to have the crew of the *Zong* charged with murder. They were never brought to justice. The slaves were legally deemed to be 'cargo', not human beings, and you can't 'murder' a pallet of baked-bean tins, can you?

There was no murder charge but, because of the outrageous insurance claim and the subsequent court case, the incident was widely reported and condemned. In 1787 the Society for Effecting the Abolition of the Slave Trade was founded and some changes were enforced. They were not radical. They were certainly not universal because no woman was allowed to join this gentlemen's club. (Another absent-minded omission by the Enlightened Ones?) The activist Thomas Clarkson set out to gather evidence of the cruelty of the trade. His most power-ful weapon proved to be a diagrammatic print. It showed a

Liverpool ship called the *Brooks* and illustrated the way it was packed with 292 Africans. The Liverpool slave traders were so worried about his activities they hired a gang to attack Clarkson as he roamed the docks there gathering stories. (He was a powerful man and escaped the thugs.)

Thanks to Clarkson's picture, in 1788 the first legal steps were taken. They were baby steps: the restrictions were not intended to abolish slavery but to simply curb overcrowding. The Slave Trade Act of 1788 placed a limit on the number of slaves that could be carried on a ship and a later amendment banned insurance cover for murdered slaves.

What Granville Sharp and Thomas Clarkson needed was representation in Parliament and that was when they persuaded William Wilberforce MP to take up their cause, which he did assiduously for the rest of his life. Greek philosopher Sextus Empiricus once wrote, 'The mills of the gods grind slowly, but they grind small.' He could have been writing about the machinery of the British Parliament. Wilberforce wasn't just battling parliamentary procedure but fierce opposition from the people who profited from the trade.

The legal defence offered by Liverpool trader James Penny would be comical if it weren't so serious a matter. Speaking about the treatment of slaves during the Atlantic crossing he said . . .

If the Weather is warm, and there appears the least sweat upon their Skins, when they come upon Deck. There are Two Men there with Cloths to rub them perfectly dry, and another to give them a little drink of fruit juice. They are then given Pipes and Tobacco. They are amused with Musical

Instruments from their own country. When tired of Music and Dancing, they then go to play Games. The slaves on our ships will sleep better than the gentlemen do on shore.

It was not the moral argument but France's slave trade with Haiti that turned the tide in favour of the abolitionists. The thinking was, 'We are at war with the French. Abolition will disrupt the French slave trade and we can use our powerful navy to enforce it.' In 1807 – twenty years after Granville Sharp and Thomas Clarkson's opening shots – the slave trade was sinking fast. The slave trade but not slavery itself was the target. British colonies kept their slaves. As late as 1814, runaway slaves were still being hanged and decapitated by the British so their heads could be hoisted on poles and their bodies gibbeted as an example to their friends. Who opposed the freeing of existing slaves? James Penny? No, it was William Wilberforce.

He argued it would be 'madness' to release slaves unprepared into the scary world of freedom and equality. He looked forward to the distant time when they could enjoy 'happy peasantry'. The campaigner Elizabeth Heyrick criticized Wilberforce's lack of ambition. Wilberforce dismissed her views because she was a woman, and her activism was 'unsuited to the female character as delineated in the Scripture.'*

Slavery was eventually banned in 1833. The slave owners received compensation. The slaves received nothing. Three days

---

* So, let's get this clear Mr Wilberforce: slaves may one day achieve freedom, but women are condemned by the Bible to eternal servitude? Nice one, Will.

after the bill was passed, Wilberforce died. He died a legend with enough statues to empty a marble mine, while statues to enslavers, like the one of Edward Colston in Bristol, are now being pulled down. But Wilberforce's sons glorified his legacy at the expense of other key campaigners like Granville Sharp, Thomas Clarkson and Elizabeth Heyrick.

No single person can rebel against slavery, but time turns people like Spartacus, Wilberforce and other humane people into symbols of the battle. Slavery still goes on covertly today. How far will you go to rebel against it?

LESSONS FROM HISTORY 4

RALLY THE TROOPS

'Let's do it. Today is a good day to die.'
CRAZY HORSE (C.1840–77) – NATIVE AMERICAN
SIOUX CHIEF

Should you ever decide to revolt then you will be helped
if you can come up with a striking turn of phrase.
Something your followers can remember and chant as
they scalp a priest or throw themselves onto the spears of
the merciless foe.

JEWISH DEFENDERS OF MASADA FORTRESS, AD 73

The Jews who rebelled against Rome fled to the near
impregnable fortress at Masada in south-east Israel. When
the Romans laid siege to the citadel, the defenders killed
themselves rather than be captured. If the alternative was
to be burnt alive, eaten alive by wild animals or thrown off
a rock alive, it's hard to blame them.

They chose ten who would kill the other 960

before killing themselves. The other 960 men, women and children cried, 'Death before slavery!' And then died to prove they believed it. There were just seven survivors – five children and two women. A caring mother took her children and hid in a water cistern. Maybe she misheard and thought the cry was 'Slavery before death'.

THE CIOMPI REVOLT, FLORENCE, 1378

The workers of Florence wanted political representation to address the high taxes and dreadful working conditions in the wool industry. The Ciompi were the wool-carders who led the protests. They identified themselves with their woollen capes and called themselves 'The Cloaks'.

They nicknamed the ruling classes 'The Hats'. Their slogan may not have been the most eloquent, but it is certainly unique: 'Death to the Hats!'

When the workers went on strike, the Hats sneered 'Get back to your cloth-making' and 'Go back and grind your pepper.' Pepper was a luxury item and an upper-class person would hand the menial task of grinding it to the serving class. This is not the level of negotiation you'd expect from your political opponent, not even in the cut and thrust of the British Parliament.

One Florentine magnate said, 'The workers are robbers and traitors, murderers and assassins, gluttons and law-breakers.' He could have added 'arsonists' because the

Cloaks started burning the houses of the Hats. At the height of their success, they even forced their way into the palace and for a while took control of the city. But their aggression upset the moderates who eventually regained power. You could say the top Hats were back.

THE PEASANTS' REVOLT, 1381

The peasants had a grievance against the landed gentry and asked, quite reasonably, who gave the lords and ladies the right to rule? It wasn't God because She had created two working-class humans: Adam who dug (or 'delved') and Eve who did a bit of spinning. (In the archaic past tense of spin, she 'span'. But try not to think of Eve as the world's first spanner.) The rebel priest, John Ball, coined the battle-cry:

> When Adam delved and Eve span,
> Who was then the gentleman?

It is of course a rhetorical question to which the answer is 'Nobody'. When rebel leader Wat Tyler was killed and the Peasants' Revolt evaporated, Ball was taken prisoner before being hanged, drawn and quartered at St Albans while the fourteen-year-old King Richard II looked on. Ball's head was displayed stuck on a pole on London Bridge. Over a span, in fact. 'The mad priest of Kent' had coined one of the best rebel cries in history.

THE FRENCH REVOLUTION, 1789

The French came up with an ideal image of post-revolutionary society with their rousing:

Liberty, equality, fraternity

It could be chanted at the foot of the guillotine as the aristos were being liberated from their heads. Of course, the French peasants weren't properly free, they certainly weren't equal – after the revolution they were poorer than ever – and according to the Bible, the world's first murder victim was killed by his brother. So although it sounded good, it might not have been too accurate.

In 1792 France went to war against Austria and the French army officer Claude Joseph Rouget de Lisle came up with a real battle hymn that exhorted the French to violence. Claiming the enemy was coming 'to cut the throats of your sons, your comrades', the hymn urged the soldiers on: 'To arms, citizens. Form your battalions, let's march, let's march, so their impure blood should water our fields'. It became the French national anthem in 1795.

Napoleon rose to power on the back of the revolution, of course. He then feared the revolutionary spirit would oust him, so he banned 'La Marseillaise'. That's irony for you.

ITALIAN REBELS, 1919

The poet Gabriele D'Annunzio (1863–1938) was an Italian MP who argued for Italy to enter the First World War. When they did, he trained as a fighter pilot at the age of fifty-two and took part in a daring raid over Austria. His squadron bombed Vienna with propaganda leaflets.

After the war he took the chance to lead his own rag-tag brigade of nationalists to seize the city of Fiume. It was a Croatian city but many Italians believed it should be part of their nation. Gabby made sure that film cameras were there to record his entry into the town. He succeeded thanks partly to his rousing battle cries of . . .

Eia, Eia, Alala

Yes, really. He said this was the cry the Greek hero Achilles had used to drive his horse forward. (His followers believed him even though Achilles was a myth.)

If 'Eia, Eia, Alala' doesn't work then you could try an English horse-driving equivalent – 'Giddy-up, Dobbin' – which has never been known to fail. (Or succeed.)

SPANISH REPUBLICAN REBELS IN THE SPANISH CIVIL WAR DURING 1937

Dolores Ibárruri – a.k.a. the Passionflower – led her Communist forces against the Spanish government forces commanded by Francisco Franco. Ibárruri divides opinion because of her Totalitarian beliefs. She may have lost the battle against Franco's Fascists but there was no doubting her ability to inspire with her oratory. Her defiant slogan lives on: 'They shall not pass.'

She borrowed it from the French General Robert Nivelle (or maybe General Philippe Pétain). He had urged his soldiers to defend Verdun with the battle-cry, 'You will not let them pass, my comrades'. This phrase, 'They shall not pass', could become a rear-window sticker in the back window of many Sunday drivers. Or maybe the cry of despairing teachers of GCSE exam pupils in some secondary schools. Dolores's other memorable rebel cry was: 'It is better to die on your feet than to live on your knees.'

Dolores didn't die on her feet. She used her feet to carry her off to the safety of Russia. When Passionflower's nemesis, General Franco, finally died of old age in 1975, she returned to Spain, a heroine, for the final fourteen years of her life. Perhaps her last slogan should have been, 'If you can't beat 'em, outlive 'em.'

TWENTIETH-CENTURY SOUTH AMERICAN REVOLUTIONS

The term 'banana republic' describes a politically unstable country, often in Central America or the Caribbean. Why? Because in the early 1900s several of these countries had their entire economy dominated by the American corporation the United Fruit Company (UFCO). The

UFCO was said to be capable of making or breaking the governments of these countries.

The resulting instability led to many revolutions and one of the iconic rebels was Che Guevara. Che was a Cuban guerrilla leader who believed a communist revolution was needed to overthrow the oppressive regimes. His philosophy is summed up in his statement: 'If mankind is ever to escape from its misery, there is only one method: the destruction of everything in fire and blood . . . there is no other way, no other hope.' So there is your cry as you go to die: fire and blood.

The fire that finished him off was gunfire; the blood was leaking out of the ends of his arms when his hands were cut off as proof that he'd been killed.

REASON TO REVOLT 5
HUNGER

*'Never did I see people under any military discipline
in such a ragged situation, the generality of them was
without shoes or stockings and scarce any clothing.
They seem to be a mob of very desperate people, and
I am creditably informed their commanders, before
they were ordered to attack any place, made them
intoxicated with spirits.'*

CORPORAL SAMUEL BLOMELEY, THE COLDSTREAM

GUARDS, ON THE IRISH REBELS – JULY 1798

Hunger is a powerful incentive to revolt. Act now or be too weak to rebel against the oppressors who are forcing you to survive on rat burgers or the occasional steak from the rump of your predeceased granny.

When famine struck in Saxon Britain, some villagers on the south coast saw the only way out was to join hands and jump off a cliff. All the cats and dogs and rats had been consumed and there was not even a morsel of hope left.

If *you* had been there you might have opted out of the jump, then let your fellow Saxons smash onto the rocks below. You'd not only survive but enjoy feasting on the fresh flesh that the carnage provided. But we aren't all as ruthless and shameless as you.

What those demoralized villagers needed was someone to blame, to rebel against. Maybe some aristocrats they could throw to their deaths as they sang, 'There'll be blue-bloods over the white cliffs of Dover'.

THE JACQUERIE, 1358 – FRENCH PEASANTS

The French are a revolting people. Where they lead it seems the rest of the world will follow. Over twenty years before the English Peasants' Revolt of 1381 the French peasants – the *Jacquerie* – were showing the way.

It started with the peasants suffering deprivation. The Hundred Years' War between France and England (1337–1453) led to the destruction of their property, pillaging of their crops and livestock as well as the disruption of the trade by which they fed themselves. How could the French king fund his army for the defence of the country? By taxing the peasants, of course.

Add to that the Black Death pandemic (1346–53) which halved the population, leading to labour shortages for the land-owners. Rather than share the hardships of the peasants, the landlords demanded higher rents from the remaining peasants. That only added to the resentment towards the wealthy elite. At this time, the peasants had no voice in the government and no way to express their grievances – except revolt.

The French rebellion was known as the *Jacquerie* because:

a) Any peasant was known as a 'Jacques' (a 'John' in English) – a very common name – so it was a revolt of the 'Johns'. Or . . .

b) they wore padded, boiled-leather jackets as a sort of cheap armour and these jackets were called 'Jacques' – so it was a revolt-of-the-padded-boiled-leather-jackets.

Take your pick. Either explanation could be right – or both could be wrong.

The *Jacquerie* weren't trained from birth to run a military operation the way the nobles were. Several nobles were murdered before anyone told them that they were a target. Killing a knight without even warning him just wasn't sporting – or chivalrous at any rate.

Inevitably a leader emerged. His name was Will Cale and he's just what the peasants needed – a strong leader *and* an experienced soldier. He was a wealthy farmer by peasant standards and came from the Beauvais region of France that was untouched by the wars against England.

Cale's followers – *les misérables* – were further disgruntled because defeat in the Battle of Poitiers in 1356 had seen their king, John II, captured by the English. What's more, the French knights had done nothing to prevent this humiliation except save their own skins. And so the *Jacquerie* armed themselves with whatever came to hand – axes, scythes and pitchforks.

A ten-thousand-strong mob captured more than a hundred castles. Some knights fled with their families – others stayed and died.

When it comes to revolting the French don't do things by halves. There's none of this lopping off the odd bishop's head. The *Jacquerie* were determined to exact the cruellest of revenges on their oppressors. There are reports of a Jacques roasting a knight on a spit, then forcing his wife to eat the roasted flesh.

The unchivalrous punishment of ladies led to an English knight and a French knight joining forces to help the town of Meaux when it suffered a Jacques-attack. John de Grailly (who was the Captal de Buch) and Gaston Phoebus united to defend the honour of the fairer sex. The knights united formed an armed force of just 120 and cut the *Jacquerie* to pieces. Pitchforks against armoured knights on horseback is what Samuel Johnson would have called 'a triumph of hope over experience'.

Once the oppressors got their act together they vowed to regain control but with a lot of spiteful revenge added to their actions. The peasant army under Cale faced the nobles near Mello. Lordly leader Charles of Navarre suggested to Cale that they should meet. There is a recurrent theme in the history of rebellion that rebel leaders believe they have achieved parity with the ruling classes when they are invited to talk. They are deluded into thinking that they have achieved enough victory that now they can lay out their demands and negotiate a peaceful settlement.

Is it a trick? Invariably, yes. Will they listen to words of caution? Usually, no. Will it end badly for the rebel? Mostly, yes.

We can only imagine what went through Cale's brain cell when he received the invite. Surely Charles of Navarre, being a knight, would abide by the rules of chivalry and treat him with respect. And Charles *would* have treated a fellow knight chivalrously. Cale, however, was not a fellow knight. He was a filthy peasant in a boiled-leather jacket who led a vicious rabble. If Cale accepted the invite to parley then he was a *stupid*, filthy peasant. Cale accepted and even went to the meeting unarmed.

On his arrival, Cale was arrested by the French nobles and locked in chains. He was tortured with a crown of red-hot iron – not really necessary but that's where the spiteful revenge played a part. He was then beheaded.

Cale's leaderless rebels were massacred. Those who survived found their conditions no better. The rich grew more extravagant in their displays of wealth as the peasants struggled against starvation. For instance, Count Robert of Artois had a park with a menagerie and aviaries, fishponds and orchards that would be the envy of any of the hungry peasants he owned. He would treat his friends to a tour of his jousting arena and pleasure garden, which had . . .

- a statue that squawked at you like a parrot
- a hosepipe that squirted water up ladies' dresses
- a trapdoor that dropped you onto a feather bed
- statues that squirted water at you as you walked past

Inside his palatial home he had a room that greeted you with a thunderstorm as you opened the door. In a word: ostentatious. His display of wealth might have aroused envy in his fellow nobles but hatred in the *Jacquerie*. Oh well – it wasn't as if the peasants were ever going to take over the country.

And that French peasants' revolt lit the way for the English to follow . . .

THE ENGLISH PEASANTS' REVOLT, 1381

The medieval feudal system is often compared to a pyramid. Monarch at the top, peasants at the bottom. If you are at the bottom, you are taking the greatest load while being crushed by it. You are a peasant, and your human rights are somewhere between zero and zilch.

William Langland (1332–86) was the presumed author of the poem *Piers Ploughman*, which depicted the life of the rural labourer graphically.

> His coat of a cloth that is thin as the East wind,
> His hood full of holes with his hair sticking through,
> His clumsy shoes, knobbled and nailed over thickly,
> Yet his toes poked clean through as he trod on the ground.
> Two miserable mittens made out of old rags,
> The fingers worn out and the filth caked on them,
> He waded in mud almost up to his ankles,
> In front are four oxen, so weary and feeble
> Their ribs could be counted, so wretched they were.

A ploughman's lot was not a happy one. And neither was his wife's. Their resentment trickled like gunpowder into a barrel and only needed a match.

As Rosa Parks (1913–2005), the American civil rights activist, put it, 'There is just so much hurt, disappointment, and oppression one can take. The line between reason and madness grows thinner.'

The peasants who had survived the Black Death had been raging on and off for thirty years and the survivors began to believe they were *special* – God's chosen ones. And that gave them a new confidence.

They became swollen with self-importance like a helium-filled balloon . . . but without the laughs. Their argument was simple. 'We surviving peasants are worth more pay. That's according to the law of supply and demand.'

But the landowners – including the Church – demurred. They had introduced a law called the Statute of Labourers in 1351. Its primary aim was to stop peasants profiting from the shortage of labour after the Black Death. Wages were limited to two pence a day. At the same time, many peasants were compelled to work, without pay, on Church land.

This Church obligation was tiresome as the peasants' time could have been used to work on their own plots. However, the power of the Church was so great that few dared to break this rule. The workers had been taught from a very early age that God would see their sins and punish them in the next life.

As well as free labour, the peasants also had to pay a tax to the Church called a tithe – a tax of 10 per cent of the value of what a family had farmed. That 10 per cent could be the difference between feast and famine for the family.

As well as labour a peasant could pay in cash or in kind (grain, animals or vegetables). The Church and the lords who owned the land sometimes demanded all three forms of payment – days of labour, a share of their produce and cash. The peasants – or villeins – never became inured to being under the well-heeled heels of the lords.

The tithes kept the peasants on the cusp of starvation and, just to rub in the fact that the Church was making a fortune, the bishops stored their ill-gotten goodies in huge tithe barns. Imagine being a hungry peasant walking on your way to your frozen field and having to walk past that barn stuffed with the bishop's food.

In some monasteries (fifty years after the Peasants' Revolt of 1381) it's been revealed that monks were five times more likely to suffer from obesity-related joint diseases than the average peasant. Monks were eating wheat-bread. Peasants in 1437–40 were trying to survive on bread made from peas or even fern roots. The fat Friar Tuck of legend was a reality.

Some of the Church grain barns, like Tithe Barn in Maidstone, are preserved as scheduled monuments. Monuments? Monuments to the oppression of the peasants?

The Peasants' Revolt began in May 1381, famously prompted by the levying of a poll tax of four pence per adult. Peasant or aristo, you all paid the same. (Girls were exempt if they were virgins. Naturally, one sergeant-at-arms, John Legge, volunteered to carry out the necessary gynaecological examinations. This is a tax avoidance check no longer practised by HMRC.) The peasants had nothing to lose if they revolted and the target was, as ever, authority, the government, the rich.

History is never as simple as a tax prompting a revolt. Another factor was a rumour that went around – a rumour that the Church did little to suppress. It said that a peasant's soul *couldn't* get into heaven because demons would refuse to carry it away. Why? Because of their horrible smell.*

With the expectation of heaven fading, the impatience for a better life NOW became more urgent. The revolt started with the philosophy that all humans are created equal – that peasants were no worse than their lordly oppressors. John Ball (1338–81), a radical priest, was the philosopher. Ball was chronicled (by his enemies) as 'the mad priest of Kent' (Froissart). But since he wasn't 'of Kent' we can challenge the 'mad' epithet too. Ball preached that as descendants of Adam and Eve all humans should be treated equally. He said, reasonably . . .

From the beginning all men by nature were created alike, and our bondage or servitude came in by the unjust oppression of naughty men. For if God would have had any bondmen from the beginning, he would have appointed who should be bond, and who free. And therefore, I exhort you to consider that now the time is come, appointed to us by God, in which ye may (if ye will) cast off the yoke of bondage, and recover liberty.

This fighting talk brought him into conflict with Simon Sudbury, Archbishop of Canterbury. Ball was thrown in jail many times. Ball, the man of ideas, needed a man of action to lead them into revolt. And that man was Wat Tyler. We don't know much about people like Wat Tyler because his followers couldn't write

---

* Who'd have thought demons could be so fussy? You too must have stood next to a few strap-hangers on the London Underground who would never get to heaven . . . or even hell.

his history . . . and his enemies weren't interested in his origins. But he must have been a compelling individual. A lion leading a ragged army of lion cubs. (Tyler/tiler was probably his occupation – roofs, not bathrooms and kitchen floors. It was not his family name.*)

As the march neared London, Wat boasted,

'In four days' time all the laws of England shall be coming from my mouth.'

Wat originated in Dartford (Kent) . . . or Maidstone or Deptford. (If there's no monument to the great man, it's because no one knows which town claims him.) He released John Ball from Maidstone jail at the start of the Peasants' Revolt.

If Thomas Jefferson later described it as watering the tree of liberty with blood, the revolting peasants would expect to see more tyrant blood than patriot blood watering the roots. As John Ball had put it succinctly, 'Now is the time.'

The time for the Peasants' Revolt to begin its predictably tragic course.

Twenty thousand revolting peasants marched on London, where they overran the Tower.

Wat's twenty thousand rebels presented their demands . . .

- No more poll tax
- No more slavery for peasants
- Freedom to use the forests
- Freedom to hunt wild animals

---

* Imagine a roofer having dreams of being a leader. A Tiler, or a Thatcher. Someone who is responsible for the Truss? National leader? It'll never happen.

They . . .

- broke into Marshalsea and Fleet prisons and set the prisoners free
- ransacked lawyers' chambers and burnt all the papers they could find
- plundered Lambeth Palace – residence of the lord chancellor – and burnt down the estate of St John's Priory
- entered the palace of the King's uncle, John of Gaunt, and threw his valuables into the Thames . . . while leaving the servants unharmed.

Terrified young king Richard II *said* he was sympathetic to the rebels. Wat Tyler believed him. Wat a mistake. The king went down the Thames on a barge to meet them but retreated when he heard their new and alarming demands: fourteen-year-old Richard was told by the rebels he must have his top fifteen advisers topped – beheaded as traitors.

Richard had a proclamation read from the Tower. It said the king would pardon the rebels if they went home and laid out their grievances in a letter. That only poured paraffin on the flames. They now wanted the heads of all the men of the chancery and the exchequer and everyone who could write a writ or a letter.

'Kill all the lawyers' was the way Shakespeare expressed it two hundred years later. The rebels also demanded they meet the king in person at Mile End: 'a fair, plain place where the people of the city did sport them in the summer season'.

Meanwhile, back at the Tower, a fearsome woman of Kent, Johanna Ferrour, led an assault on the fortress where their main targets were cowering, the chancellor/Archbishop of Canterbury (Simon Sudbury) and treasurer (Robert Hales*).

In court documents Johanna was described as 'Chief perpetrator and leader of rebellious evildoers from Kent'.

She was also accused of burning the Savoy Palace – the grandest house in London at the time – and stealing a chest of gold.

Incidentally, Johanna was never convicted and may have returned to the peaceful life as a housewife in Rochester. But she had left her mark – a rare female footnote in the pages of history.

There were guards at the Tower, but clearly not sturdy beefeaters because they simply opened the gates and let Johanna and her friends in. (Or did they? Some say Richard II told the guards to let them in so Sudbury and Hales would be sacrificial scapegoats and save him having to give them the trial the rebels demanded.)

> And at last they found the Archbishop of Canterbury, Simon
> Sudbury, a valiant man and a wise, and chief chancellor of
> England, and a little before he had said mass before the king.
> These gluttons took him and strake off his head, and also,
> they beheaded the lord of Saint John's and a friar minor,
> master in medicine, they slew him in despite of his master,
> and a sergeant at arms called John Leg.†

---

* Hales was hated as the tax-collector in chief. If you are looking for a model of understatement, the chronicler Thomas Walsingham described him as a 'Magnanimous knight, though the commons loved him not'.

† Yes, that Sir John Legge, the king's tax collector and virgin inspector for Kent. A sergeant-at-*arms* called *Leg*? Once the Tower fell he was out on a limb.

The archbishop had his head forced onto an executioner's block. It took eight blows to hack through his neck. Clearly the peasants hadn't had a lot of practice at the decapitation lark. That must have hurt. His mitre was then nailed to his head . . . which wouldn't hurt at all.

> And these four heads were set on four long spears and they made them to be borne before them through the streets of London and at last set them a-high on London bridge, as though they had been traitors to the king and to the realm.

The archbishop's head was stuck on London Bridge. (For the ghouls among you, his skull can still be seen at the church of St Gregory at Sudbury in Suffolk. As Archbishop of Canterbury, his noggin can literally be seen as head of the church.)

Hales's head joined Sudbury's. As treasurer, he took a large portion of the blame for the introduction of the Poll Tax. That was a bit unfair as the taxes had been passed shortly before Hales became treasurer. But no one worried about fairness.

On 15 June 1381, along with Mayor of London William Walworth, Richard II rode out to meet Wat and his peasant followers. Tyler made his demands. The principal demand was an end to serfdom – a dismantling of the feudal pyramid. The people of England should be free to buy or rent their own land, buy and sell their own goods, and have the right to take their grievances, gripes and grumbles to the king's court.

The rebels repeated the call for the execution of their oppressors while the rebels themselves would be granted an amnesty. Richard was equivocal about the executions – the alleged traitors would have fair trials. But apart from that, he appeared to cave in to their ultimatums.

The *Anonimalle Chronicle* (probably written by a monk from York) said . . .

> To this the King gave an easy answer and said that he [Tyler] should have all that he could fairly grant, reserving only for himself the regality of his crown. And then he bade him go back to his home, without making further delay.

An unlikely victory was on the cards.

The story of his demise is well known: when Tyler went to meet young King Richard II, an argument broke out between Tyler and some of the royal servants. Mayor Walworth ordered Tyler to be arrested. Wat tried to evade arrest and that was Walworth's excuse to stab the rebel leader.

King Richard II looked on. This was the young man who had promised his subjects a peaceful resolution. The resolution was Tyler's death, and the morale of the rebels dissolved.

When the peasants had been sent back to their homes, Ball was taken prisoner. He was hanged, drawn and quartered at St Albans in the presence of Richard II. His head was stuck on a pike on London Bridge, just as Archbishop Sudbury's had been . . . in fact Sudbury's dead head would have been removed to make way for his enemy's. Sudbury would have enjoyed that. The quarters of Ball's body were displayed at four different towns. There was to be no forgiving and forgetting.

As English movie director Alfred Hitchcock (1899–1980) said, 'Revenge is sweet . . . and not fattening.'

The revolt was suppressed brutally, and Richard went back on all his promises. Yet the peasant actions had demonstrated the power of collective action. There were some improvements in the peasant life. The feudal system had been irrevocably weakened and the lords became more cautious about how they treated their peasants. The peasants' labour was a commodity that could be used for bargaining, not taken for granted. The road to change was a one-way street to improvement for the masses.

The English Peasants' Revolt was a failure and a success.

THE IRISH FAMINE, 1845

There is a folk memory of the past that is just as important as written chronicles. Folk memory is passed down through generations by word of mouth, songs, stories, traditions and superstitions.

Famines like the 1845 tragedy in Ireland can leave communities too weak to rise in revolt. But folk memories can last hundreds or thousands of years, and sometimes the descendants of the victims exact revenge generations later. In this case it was eighty years before the Irish finally threw off the British rule.

The Irish of the Little Ice Age in 1315 suffered hunger and the depredations of Scottish invaders. They never did rebel against the famines the way the poor folk did in England and in France. But that folk memory haunted the peasants till the more famous famine of 1845. An Irish sufferer reported . . .

We ate the dogs first, then the donkeys, the horses, foxes, badgers, hedgehogs and even frogs. We stewed nettles and dandelions and collected all the nuts and berries we could find. The people on the coast could eat shellfish but a lot of them were poisonous. Maybe it was better a quick death from poisoning than a slow one from hunger.

The British overlords were the target of Irish loathing and not without reason. Treasury official Charles Trevelyan was the man responsible for organizing famine relief. Yet he didn't hide the fact that he thought that the famine was God's way of punishing the Irish. He believed in minimal government intervention, self-regulation by the peasants and public works to provide waged labour for the starving natives. Despite their weakened state he must have imagined they'd be fit to build an HS2-type line from Belfast to Cork (it being a long way to Tipperary).

Trevelyan claimed that 'the real evil with which we have to contend is not the physical evil of the Famine but the moral evil of the selfish, perverse and turbulent character of the people'.

Don't pull your punches, Charlie. Tell us what you really think. The Irish had to witness boatloads of homegrown oats and grain shipped to England. The English absentee landlords put profits first. The government didn't want to interfere in 'the market' and upset those influential landlords. The Irish peasants had no votes, no power . . . and no food.

Food riots broke out in places such as Youghal, near Cork, where the starving populace tried to confiscate a boatload of grain. At Dungarvan, County Waterford, British troops shot into a protesting crowd, killing at least two people and wounding several others. The crowd was armed with stones. Small wonder that this rebellion ended before it began.

A million died in the famine. Charles Trevelyan's aversion to helping the Irish is in contrast to his support for famine-hit Scots in their Highland potato famine. There, he said, 'The people must not, under any circumstances, be allowed to starve.' One law for the Scots and another for the Irish. In the twenty-first-century fashion for historical apologies, there has been no reparation for the inhumanities of the Trevelyan treatment of the Irish in the famine. However, in 2024 Laura Trevelyan, a BBC journalist, apologized for her family's involvement in the slave trade in Grenada and offered reparations. It seems the family has a lot to say sorry for.

The hunger was passing, but resentment at the British government's inadequate response wasn't. 1848 saw the outbreak of rebellions and revolutions across Europe – 'the springtime of the people'. That inspired William Smith O'Brien to form his protest group, 'The Young Irelanders', which believed an independent Ireland could have managed the famine better. Like many rebel leaders, O'Brien was born into a wealthy landowning family. He served as a Member of Parliament. O'Brien called for peaceful protest, but the panicking government tried to suppress protest of any kind, which ironically persuaded the Young Irelanders that armed insurrection was the only course open to them.

Inspired by the French, they erected barricades in the village of The Commons to await the arrival of the police and the military. When the first cohort of constables arrived and saw the barricades they didn't fancy a confrontation, so they turned aside. The rebels perceived that as weakness – which it probably was – and chased the craven constabulary across the fields. (Images of the Keystone Cops spring to mind.) The forty-seven-strong police contingent took shelter in a large five-storey farmhouse. They covered themselves with yet more glory by taking the five young children of the house as hostages. O'Brien's rebels surrounded the house. The owner of the house, and mother of the children, Widow Margaret McCormack, asked to be allowed inside. The cowardly cops refused.

O'Brien went to the farmhouse window to negotiate and even shook hands with some of the polite police. But one officer fired at him. The angry rebels returned fire, leading to a two-hour gunfight. Two rebels were fatally shot. When police reinforcements finally arrived, the rebels melted away.

This feeble famine rebellion became disparagingly known as 'The battle of the Widow McCormack's Cabbage Garden'. Some revolts end not with a bang but a whimper. The Young Irelanders were eventually rounded up and most were transported to Australia or Bermuda. O'Brien was sentenced to death but the government in Britain knew the danger of making martyrs, so he joined his acolytes in Australia. When he returned with a conditional pardon five years later, he remained an advocate for nationalism, but never attempted a rerun of the cabbage-patch putsch.

The bitter folk memory would finally be exorcised in December 1921 when Éire gained independence from the United Kingdom. An Anglo-Irish Treaty was signed which formally ended the Irish War of Independence. The Irish Free State then became a Republic in 1949. The cabbage-patch heroes would have enjoyed seeing their long struggle reach a successful conclusion.

LESSONS FROM HISTORY 5

GATHER INTELLIGENCE

'It is ten thousand times cheaper to pay the best spies lavishly than even a tiny army poorly.'
SUN TZU (FIFTH CENTURY BC) – CHINESE GENERAL AND STRATEGIST

If you want to revolt but don't want to storm a palace then you may like to take a less direct and physical approach. You can spy for your cause. It still has its dangers, of course because you run the risk of execution if you are caught. Maybe a little torture first till you succumb to the red-hot pincers, the rack and the thumbscrews. But if you're not prepared to lose your fingernails for the revolution yet, take heart from your brave predecessors who blazed a trail for you.

Lydia Barrington Darragh is typical of the pacifists who helped to rebel without using violence. Lydia was from Dublin, Ireland but moved to Philadelphia in the 1750s. Her family were non-combatant Quakers, but they sided with the Patriots during the American Revolution. During the occupation of Philadelphia, some high-ranking

British soldiers were quartered in the Darraghs' home. Darragh regularly spied on the soldiers' meetings under the pretext of bringing them refreshments or wood for the fire. Darragh's husband, William, wrote the information she uncovered in a special shorthand which Lydia stitched into cloth-covered buttons on her son John's coat. John then took the message to his older brother, Charles, who was serving in the Continental Army under General Washington.

As Abigail, the wife of John Adams (the second US president) said, 'If particular care and attention is not paid to the ladies, we are determined to foment a rebellion and will not hold ourselves bound by any laws in which we have no voice or representation.'

Not all revolutionaries march along public streets waving massive flags. Sometimes, they are hiding in plain sight.

MITHRIDATES THE GREAT, 132–63 BC

In 120 BC Mithridates was prince of Pontus (a northern part of modern day Turkey). It's likely his mother poisoned his father to put his brother Chrestus on the throne. Mithridates was older than Chrestus, so of course their mother also tried to have Mithridates assassinated . . . several times.

Mithridates fled from the assassins and wisely disguised himself as a beggar. He learnt twenty-two languages by the age of fourteen – always useful for a spy – and wandered through Turkish cities studying their defences.

After a few years he knew all about those defences and the weaknesses of the cities. He only needed to gather a small army to overrun the cities. Before long, his power was so great he was able to return to Pontus and reclaim the throne. Mithridates's mother died in prison, and Chrestus was executed. To consolidate his power, he married his sister. That's a strategy you may not want to emulate. As the English conductor Sir Thomas Beecham (1879–1961) once said, 'Try everything once except incest and Morris dancing.'

KING ALFRED THE GREAT (AD 849–99)

Alfred was the leader of the Saxons in England at a time when the Danes were taking over the country. Like Mithridates he was forced into hiding. If he was going to revolt against the Danish forces he needed to know more about their strengths. One story says that Alfred disguised himself as a minstrel and wandered into the Danish camp. He entertained them and stayed to their feast where they talked about their battle plans. The next day, Alfred slipped out of the camp and prepared the Saxon army using his intel to defeat the plans he'd overheard. This story was first written down five hundred years after Alfred's death, so there's no way of checking if it's true. You'd have to ask how Alfred, as a minstrel, learnt to recite Norse sagas in Danish and not be discovered. But why let common sense get in the way of a good story?

CHRISTOPHER MARLOWE (1564–93)

The playwright could have been as great as William Shakespeare. The trouble is he seemed to enjoy spying as much as writing. He worked for Elizabeth I's spymaster, Sir Francis Walsingham, and his job was to uncover Catholic plots against the queen. Like many other spies, his masters suspected he was working secretly for the enemy – in this case, the Catholics. Was Marlowe a rebel-crusher or a revolutionary? A double-crossing double-agent? In a meeting with three of Walsingham's spies, Marlowe got into a fight, was stabbed in the eye and died. The spies claimed it was a quarrel about the bill – the 'reckoning'. Some historians think Marlowe was executed because his spymasters mistrusted him. Certainly, the inquest hastily accepted the 'self defence' explanation and the killer was never punished. Was that because the killer was acting on orders from Walsingham?

DANIEL DEFOE (1660–1731)

This English writer was not popular with the government because he wrote offensive things about them. After a spell in prison he offered to work for the government and train its spies. These spies would report on exactly who was making trouble in Britain. The idea was to scotch any revolts before they started. Defoe's secret agents were trained to mix with the population and seem quite ordinary – then betray their friends. Defoe was able to give

up spying when one of his books became a great success —
the famous *Robinson Crusoe*. It's a book you should
consider nominating if you are ever invited on to *Desert
Island Discs*.

BENJAMIN FRANKLIN (1706–90)

The famous scientist tried to be a double agent. He
was one of the founders of the American spy network
and pretended to be working for them in the War of
Independence. In fact he was passing on their secrets to
the British. Then, when it was clear that the Americans
were going to win the war, he quietly joined the American
side. The man was eminently sensible and survived to
become a hero of American science. One of the American
leaders, John Quincy Adams, had suspected Franklin
of betraying his country but he didn't have enough hard
evidence. That's an important lesson: if you are going to
hop on and off the revolution bus, don't leave evidence.

ANNA SMITH STRONG (1740–1812)

Anna of Setauket, New York was an American Patriot,
and she was one of what may have been very few female
members of the Culper Spy Ring during the American
Revolution. Her perceived main contribution in the
ring was to relay signals to a courier who ran smuggling
operations and military missions for General George
Washington. Anna would arrange clothes on her

clothesline as a means of signalling the location of hidden documents to fellow spy Caleb Brewster. Six coves along the shore of Long Island had been designated as dead-drop locations. The number of handkerchiefs hung corresponded to one of the six coves.

As with Franklin, no information has been found concerning Anna's activities after the war other than that she and her husband, Selah Strong III, lived quietly in Setauket for the rest of their lives. Sounds like they had a real Bond.

SIR ROBERT BADEN-POWELL (1857–1941)

From 1880 till 1902 this army officer used his skill as an actor to enter enemy territory in disguise – in Herzegovina he pretended to be a butterfly collector while collecting plans of enemy gun positions, and in Hamburg he pretended to be a drunk to get details of German warships.

The First Boer War broke out in 1880 when Dutch settlers in South Africa – the Boers – rebelled against British control of Transvaal, winning an unexpected victory and regaining their independence. Tensions soon escalated again, leading to another full-scale conflict. In the Second Boer War (1899–1902) Baden-Powell became a spy-trainer, using Zulus to spy on the Dutch, and this time the British came out on top. Baden-Powell wrote a book called *Aids to Scouting* in 1899 and it was used to train boy-soldiers. This later gave him the idea of creating the Boy

Scout organization and that's what he is remembered for. But he was a spy first.

MATA HARI (1876–1917)

The Dutch woman Mata Hari was a very popular dancer in the early 1900s and had many high-ranking admirers. Mata Hari was able to learn French and British secrets and was accused of selling them to Germany during the First World War. Mata Hari offered to work for the French Secret Service, but they accused her of betraying them. The French put her on trial, and she was sentenced to death by firing squad. She bravely refused to have a blindfold. Defiant to the end, she denied espionage was her motive. 'A harlot? Yes, but a traitress, never.' The truth, which didn't emerge until after she died, is that she never learnt any dangerous secrets and never betrayed anyone. So you should always try to make sure you don't look like a spy, particularly when you really are.

REASON TO REVOLT 6
DECEPTION

'*Every man has his own courage and is betrayed because he seeks in himself the courage of other persons.*'
RALPH WALDO EMERSON (1803–82) – AMERICAN
PHILOSOPHER

Throughout history rebels have been misled and betrayed. Promises of support or weapons fail to materialize and people you thought were allies show their true colours. The would-be royal assassin Guy Fawkes, for instance, saw the Gunpowder Plot betrayed by an anonymous letter to the authorities. The letter was sent to Lord Monteagle, alerting him . . .

Out of concern for your safety, I advise you to avoid attending the upcoming Parliament. A great punishment is planned, and there will be a terrible blow dealt during the session and yet they shall not see who hurts them. Don't ignore this warning but excuse yourself and go to the countryside for safety.

The identity of the traitor with inside information remains a mystery, but Monteagle passed this message on. The authorities instituted a search of the Houses of Parliament, on the night of 4 November. (Yes, we know the old rhyme tells us to remember the fifth of November, but Fawkes was arrested on the fourth.)

James I himself authorized the use of torture in a warrant: 'If he will not other ways confess, the gentler tortures are first to be used upon him, and then step by step you may employ the harsher, and so speed your good work.' Guy Fawkes, far from betraying his co-conspirators, held out bravely for three months under torture on the rack. He wanted to give his comrades the opportunity to escape. His courageous attempt failed to save his accomplices, but he wasn't to know that.

Monteagle – and the writer of the letter – may have cost the rebels their lives, but on the other hand they saved hundreds of others. That is the justification of most deceivers.

LAMBERT SIMNEL AND PERKIN WARBECK – PRETENDERS TO HENRY VII'S THRONE, 1487 AND 1491

The world is awash with conspiracy theories. You know the sort of thing: Elvis Presley faked his death to avoid a Mafia plot and has been seen caring for a hound dog in the ghetto at the back of Heartbreak Hotel. Aliens built the pyramids and Stonehenge because humans couldn't. Reptilian humanoids (in disguise as our world leaders) are now controlling humanity, taking the occasional holiday to abduct real humans from lonely country roads.

These barely credible tales have been with us for centuries and are still believed today. The thing about conspiracy theories is that, no matter how preposterous they may be, there will be some people (often many people) who believe them to be true. A sensible person (like you) may see the absurdity so why do your fellow-humans cling on to them? Because they want them to be true. If it isn't all a big conspiracy, the alternative is to accept that no one knows what they're doing, and that's really scary.

One of the most lasting sources of conspiracy is the fate of the so-called 'Princes in the Tower'. In 1483 King Richard III usurped the throne that was rightly his twelve-year-old nephew Edward's. Richard III was a savvy politician and knew that his enemies could use little Edward as a rallying point for a rebellion. Edward was offered safe accommodation in the palace known as the Tower of London. He had his brother, Richard, Duke of York, aged nine, for company. As long as they lived they were an existential threat to Richard III. They 'disappeared', which was convenient for the king; in fact, it was so convenient our sensible reader (like you) will agree that it is pretty certain Richard III had the princes killed.

Richard III died two years later at the Battle of Bosworth Field, the last in the three-hundred-year Plantagenet line. A new dynasty, the Tudors, took over. They would have been vulnerable to any resurgence of the Plantagenet family like the Princes in the Tower, but conveniently they weren't around any more.

Later, the playwright William Shakespeare wanted to suck up to his Tudor sponsors. He wrote a play about Richard III in which the dead Plantagenet was not simply a shrewd and ruthless politician but an inhuman monster capable of murdering children under his protection.* Shakespeare's Richard III died with the cry, 'A horse, a horse, my kingdom for a horse,' because it scanned nicely in iambic pentameter and Shakespeare needed to explain why there was no armoured war horse on stage. A more likely source says he died crying, 'Treason, treason' ... which it was.

It's a curious facet of human nature that the more you blacken someone's character the more people will leap to their defence. Down the years many people have argued that Richard III was such a delightful bloke that he would never have had those princes eliminated. He has been defamed and is innocent. They say Shakespeare was a Tudor lackey who knew which side his bread was buttered. The last may be true ... but it doesn't mean Richard III was innocent.

The princes may have been out of the picture but, as predicted, there were challengers to the Tudor throne. Lambert Simnel came first, in 1487. Disgruntled Yorkist supporters, led by John de la Pole, Earl of Lincoln, started to plot against the Tudor victor, King Henry VII. They found a Prince Edward lookalike, Lambert Simnel, to impersonate Edward Plantagenet. Simnel was the son of a joiner from Oxford. But Richard III had never declared the Princes in the Tower to be dead, so the rebel phony was almost credible.

The plotters were backed by Richard III's sister, Margaret of Burgundy, who funded the recruitment of German mercenaries. There was also support from the Irish nobility who were

---

* If Shakespeare had been a bit more imaginative Richard could have been revealed to be a reptilian humanoid in disguise.

traditionally more supportive of the Yorkist cause. They quickly crowned Simnel in Dublin.

The rebel army of Irish troops and German mercenaries landed in Lancashire, anticipating that the disgruntled English public would flock to their banner. It was a disappointment. The English may not have liked the Tudor but after thirty years of ruinous Wars of the Roses they favoured peace over more upheaval.

Simnel's rebel leaders changed their strategy and went for bust. Instead of marching in hope on London they aimed to confront Henry VII's army on the battlefield. On 16 June 1487, the armies met at Stoke Field in Nottinghamshire. The battle was bitter, but at the end of the day the rebels were defeated, and John de la Pole was killed.

Lambert Simnel was spared execution because of his age. Lambert became a faithful servant to Henry VII and, in time, was promoted to become the falconer to Henry VII's son, King Henry VIII. He was still alive forty years after the Battle of Stoke.

The uprising may have failed, but the principle of choosing a decoy duck to give a rebellion some focus was still a sound one. Perkin Warbeck emerged a few years later, in 1491. Lambert Simnel had claimed to be Prince Edward so the next pretender had to be his younger brother, Richard of York, who would by now be a teenager – around seventeen years old. The pawn chosen to depose the king was known in Flanders as Pierrechon de Werbecque, and his backers were France and Burgundy, who wanted to destabilize the Tudors. Perkin said that he ('Richard of York') had been spared by the executioners who killed his older brother Edward, and smuggled off to Flanders. It was important to confirm that Edward was dead because that made Richard of York the legitimate Plantagenet heir, of course.

The attempts to put Perkin on the throne came and failed regularly in the 1490s. The old reliables, Margaret of Burgundy and the Irish, backed him. Perkin tried to invade in 1495 (Kent), 1496 (Scotland) and 1497 (Cornwall). On the third attempt, Warbeck was captured. He was taken to the Tower after being paraded through the streets to cries of derision from the Cockney commoners.

This pretender was old enough to face execution but, again, Henry Tudor treated him with mercy, even inviting Warbeck to feasts, albeit under guard. Warbeck could have lived happily ever after, like Simnel. But he attempted to escape from the royal court; he was locked in the Tower and tried to escape again. The tiresome and deluded young man had tried Henry VII's patience and was sentenced to death. He didn't get the axe like a nobleman; he was hanged as a commoner.

If the support from France had been to destabilize the English throne then in a way it came close to success. Henry VII had shaky finances and the defence against Warbeck's pitiful invasions cost his exchequer £13 million in today's money. Still, the Tudors survived another hundred years. The Princes in the Tower had not survived, and the conspiracy theories remained delusional. In fact, in 1674, workmen at the Tower of London found a wooden box under a staircase which contained two small human skeletons. The bones were widely accepted at the time as those of the princes. Modern DNA testing could prove it, but the authorities won't give permission.

Richard III could have nullified the pretenders' claims if he had only said, 'Yes, I had them bumped off and buried the little beggars under a staircase.' His failure to confess caused a lot of grief for his killer, Henry VII, so that would have pleased him. The mystery bones ended up in Westminster Abbey after a respectful reburial. As they were dumped under the staircase we can imagine their little spirits cried out, 'A hearse, a hearse, my kingdom for a hearse.'

Or is that a conspiracy theory too far?

REVOLUTIONARY WOMEN, 1793

Olympe de Gouges was one of the most extraordinary women in the French Revolution, and also one of the most honourable. While others like Robespierre and Napoleon climbed to the top of the tree of self-interest, Olympe was an idealist. Her fate in 1793 attracted one anonymous observer to record it:

Yesterday at seven in the evening a most remarkable woman called Olympe de Gouges was taken to the scaffold. She held the distinguished title, 'Woman of letters'.

She walked to the scaffold with a calm and composed expression and the executioners, who had driven her to this place, were forced to admit they had never seen such courage and beauty before. This woman had embraced the revolution, but having seen how vile the Jacobin system was she chose to disavow her former comrades. She tried to expose the rogues through her writings which she had printed and published. They never forgave her, and she paid for her recklessness with her head.

Having welcomed the revolutionary cry of 'Liberty, fraternity and equality' she was disillusioned to discover 'fraternity' was interpreted literally as 'brotherhood'. Women need not apply. 'Equality' and 'liberty' were equally revealed as revolutionary rewards for *les hommes*.

Maybe Olympe was naive to expect women of the French Revolution to overturn thousands of years spent in the second-class compartment of life.

The starting pistol that set off the French Revolution had been fired on 14 July 1789 when the *sans-culottes* (trouserless) mob attacked the Bastille prison. The tabloid rags of the time later said that attack was led by a woman – Anne-Josèphe Théroigne de Méricourt.

Anne-Josèphe was certainly a passionate advocate of revolution and attended the revolutionary meetings. Typically, she had to dress as a man to seek parity and (equally typical) she was derided by her nervous opponents as 'ugly'. It's true that she had a pronounced squint but not many male heroes of history would win contests for their looks. Her opponents also tried to discredit her as a woman of loose morals who slept with every single one of the new National Assembly. That would have been 576 fellers at an average of three a day if it had been true . . . which of course it wasn't.

Anne-Josèphe was as tall and wild-haired as Boudica as she reputedly led the attack on the symbol of royal privilege, the Bastille. There were just seven prisoners incarcerated there but what mattered was the symbolism, not the statistics. And just as important was the prison's supply of gunpowder, which the republicans wanted to get their hands on.

The defenders were overwhelmed and the governor Bernard-René Jourdan de Launay was dragged off to face a revolutionary court. He never made it. (Since 'trigger warnings' are in fashion, may I suggest that readers of a delicate disposition may opt to skip the next paragraph?)

In the streets, de Launay was beaten and stabbed repeatedly till he cried, 'Enough. Let me die.' They obliged but not before he lashed out and kicked an unemployed cook named Desnot in the groin. After that, the skills of a Parisian artisan were employed when the butcher Mathieu Jouve Jourdan was called upon to saw off de Launay's head. The head was paraded around the city for hours and finally deposited in the Seine.

This action was allegedly led by the Amazonian terrorist Anne-Josèphe. A closer look at her history reveals she wasn't even in Paris at the time of the Bastille attack. When she did arrive she soon became disillusioned with the failure of women to be granted equality. The women who supported her political opponents attacked her in the street, lifted her dress and whipped her bare backside. This sisterly betrayal destroyed her mental health. She was declared insane and spent ten years in an asylum, living in squalor.

If Anne-Josèphe Théroigne de Méricourt was the poster-girl for action (largely apocryphal) then Olympe de Gouges provided the intellectual challenge to the women's cause. She was a pro-lific writer of plays and pamphlets and a champion of equality for women. She hit the same brick wall as Anne-Josèphe. One political activist, the Marquis de Sade, summed up the male view when he wrote, 'The natural inferiority of women to men is universally evident.' Sade himself, arrested for writing pornographic novels, is not the credible source of any opinion, let alone on female rights. In fact, when he was arrested and threatened with the guillotine, his revolutionary zeal evaporated and he was released to die in an asylum like Anne-Josèphe.

Olympe de Gouges deserves to be remembered as a woman who died for her beliefs. Olympe was an advocate for allowing women to enlist to fight for the Republic when it went to war with Austria and Prussia. That proposal was defeated. No surprise there, as the Marquis de Sade and his 'superior' male mates voted against her. Olympe railed at women as much as the men: 'Oh, women, women, when will you cease to be blind? What gains have you made from the Revolution? Whatever barriers they set up against you it is in your power to conquer them. You only have to want it.' Ah, if only that were true. 'Why can't women live equal to me?' she argued. 'If a woman commits a crime she will die equal to a man.' Prophetic.

In 1793 Queen Marie Antoinette died, equal to a man. Olympe argued for a monarchy, properly regulated by the people, a bit like Britain today. It was a suicidal thing to propose, and she was arrested by Robespierre's Terror police. On the surface her crime was to have revolted against the revolution. In fact, it was her feminism that the Terror wanted to silence.

And so she went to the guillotine, defiant and unapologetic to the end. Five days later the writer and revolutionary Madame Roland followed Olympe to the National Razor accused of defying the ban on women engaging in politics. She cried out from the scaffold: 'Oh liberty, what crimes are committed in your name?'

The women of the 1790s had been deceived: persuaded to support the quest for freedoms that they were never going to win for themselves. Betrayed by men. Taking liberties.

JEREMIAH BRANDRETH – THE PENTRICH REVOLUTION, 1817

If you are in power then you've probably acquired a taste for it. You want to remain in power. There is growing discontent with your rule, but you can't quite identify the would-be leaders. What do you do? You instigate a revolt against your authority. The rebel leaders will come out into the open so you can dispose of them. Not only that but you can punish them severely and make a show of what will happen to the next person to contemplate your overthrow. Cracking idea.

Naturally you can't go out and stir up trouble yourself. You need someone to do it for you. That person will be a devious slimeball, a ruthless and treacherous rat. That sounds a bit harsh on the job advert. It sounds much better cloaked in an eloquent French phrase. Yes, let's call our infiltrating piece of scum an *agent provocateur*. Yes, that sounds much more acceptable.

William Shakespeare's character Hamlet said, 'When sorrows come, they come not single spies, but in battalions.' In reality, it would be better to say, 'When spies come, they come not in battalions but bring sorrows.' And that's what agent provocateur William J. Oliver brought to Britain in 1817.

Oliver was about forty years old and described by the *Leeds Mercury* in June 1817 as . . .

a person of genteel appearance and good address, nearly six feet high, of erect figure, light hair, red and rather large whiskers, and a full face, a little pitted with the small-pox. His usual dress was a light fashionable coloured brown coat, black waistcoat, dark-blue mixture pantaloons, and Wellington boots.*

The Napoleonic Wars ended at Waterloo in 1815, but instead of the British recession ending as the Luddite protests faded, things just got worse for the underclasses. With the demobilization of Napoleonic troops, more men were chasing jobs and creating mass unemployment. Taxes were raised to pay the war debt, so the cost of living went up as incomes fell. New Corn Laws were enforced to keep grain prices high to favour the rich landowners. Those Corn Laws made imported corn expensive, even when homegrown supplies were short. And, as it happened, a cold, wet winter in 1816 meant British corn was in short supply.

The price of bread rose. Discontent grew. The Spa Fields riots in Middlesex erupted with the averred aim of taking over the government, the Tower of London and the Bank of England. A placard at the meeting claimed . . .

Four Millions in Distress . . .
Four Millions Embarrassed . . .
One Million-and-half fear Distress . . .
Half-a-million live in splendid Luxury . . .

---

* The riding boots the Duke of Wellington liked to wear, not rubber wellies.

Death would now be a relief to Millions
Arrogance, Folly, and Crimes – have brought affairs to this
   dread Crisis.

In March 1817, around 25,000 textile workers met in Manchester and several hundred of them set off to petition the Prince Regent in London. (They clearly had no faith in parliamentary democracy.) The King's Dragoon Guards pursued them and several sabre chops later the march was broken up. Only one man reached London with his petition, and the new Seditious Meetings Act was passed that month. What constituted 'sedition', you might ask? Well, like 'treason', pretty much anything the lord lieutenants of the counties fancied really.

'Tranquillity and harmony', were the watchwords of the prime minister, Lord Liverpool. He urged the home secretary, Lord Sidmouth, to use 'tranquillity and harmony' to smash the Luddites, grind the revolutionaries into the soil and hang anyone who so much as talked of sedition. You can just hear him: 'Tranquillity and harmony, Sidmouth. That's the ticket, old chap.'

Around the same time, William J. Oliver toured the disaffected Midlands from Barnsley to Birmingham and spoke passionately of a march on London. William preached revolution yet made some remarkable escapes from arrest when rebel meetings were raided by troops. He ended up in Derbyshire where he met the leader of the out-of-work stocking-makers, Jeremiah Brandreth. Oliver brought Brandreth encouraging news, he said. From his travels he could confirm that fifty thousand men were marching to London to storm the Tower. Brandreth's own group of protestors should join the march.

The 'revolution' began on 9 June. Brandreth had held a rallying meeting at a pub in the village of Pentrich, the White Horse. He told his supporters he'd lead them on a march to Nottingham. He had been told that other marchers would join them en route. On reaching Nottingham 'they would receive 100 guineas, bread, meat and ale'. William J. Oliver had promised all that. They would then lead an attack on the local militia barracks and arm themselves. Along with William J. Oliver's phantom army of fifty thousand they would overthrow the government and 'overthrow poverty for ever'.

At 10 p.m. on 9 June, in heavy rain, the marchers left the pub and set out armed with scythes, pitchforks, sticks and a few guns. They knocked on farm doors and tried to force men to join them, but there was resistance. During one argument the servant Robert Walters was fatally shot.

They went on to Butterley Ironworks and demanded arms and cannon-shot but the Butterley men refused. The rebels stopped at three public houses along the way, and promised to pay landlords ... after the government had fallen. Many men defected – well, it was raining – but a small band made it across the border into Nottinghamshire at around dawn. There, they came face to face with a detachment of the King's Hussars. There was a brief scuffle, some marchers were arrested and more disappeared into the breaking morning. A report described them as 'a picture of despair and wretchedness, none of them seeming to be above the rank of labourers or working mechanics'.

A grand jury – of landowners, slave-owners and industrialists – decided the labourers and working mechanics would face charges of treason. A show trial in October was a national sensation, especially when the ringleaders were sentenced to the traditional traitor's death:

> To be drawn on a hurdle to the place of execution and there be hanged by the neck, but not until they are dead, but that they should be taken down again, and that when they are yet alive their bowels should be taken out and burnt before their faces, and that afterwards their heads should be severed from their bodies, and their bodies be divided into four quarters, and their heads and quarters to be at the King's disposal.

The sentence was commuted to hanging then beheading after death. Small mercies. Fourteen other rebels were transported to Australia, and six more jailed.

There was debate in the press about the rights and wrongs of the 'example' being made of Pentrich men. The houses where the guilty men had lived were pulled down, as was the White Horse meeting place. Wives and children were put out of their homes. Land taken from guilty men was redistributed to loyal tenants, some of whom had given evidence against them at the trial. The call for reform was silenced and it was to be almost twenty more years before reform was achieved.

And William J. Oliver who urged them on to their deaths? He wasn't around when the marchers set off through the Nottingham rain. Are we surprised? Probably not.

As you've probably guessed, William 'The Spy' Oliver was a government plant. He had presented himself to the Home Office on 28 March 1817, offering his services as an informer. Sidmouth accepted his offer. William was vilified for his role in the Pentrich riot and wisely decamped to South Africa where he spent the rest of his life.

Liverpool and Sidmouth had what they wanted. Power stayed in the hands of the privileged.

Treason? Or judicial murder?

MOUNT A PROTEST

'Any people anywhere being inclined and having the power have the right to rise up and shake off the existing government and form a new one that suits them better.'

MAO ZEDONG (1893–1976) – CHAIRMAN OF THE CHINESE COMMUNIST PARTY

You (hypothetically) want to protest? What methods are at your disposal? You may choose to fight them on the beaches with bombs and bullets but you'd have a hard job finding an insurance company to give you a life policy. Or you may opt for a more courageous tactic like writing a strongly worded email to your MP. That way you could save the world *and* save yourself the crippling cost of a postage stamp. Be aware though that while your pen may be mightier than the sword, even the simple act of publishing a rebellious missive can have its dangers if history is anything to go by.

Even failed revolts can be useful because they could teach you what *not* to do when you rise up against your oppressors, against injustice or against that traffic warden who didn't believe the DOCTOR ON CALL sign in your windscreen.

Is there ever such a thing as a 'peaceful protest'? Or is it as illusory as a 'victimless crime'?

PAMPHLETS – JOHN STUBBS FRENCH MARRIAGE PAMPHLET, 1579

Get your message out there in print. You can preach from a pulpit, but the power of the printed word is prime. Put yourself in Tudor England. Queen Elizabeth I is being courted by the French Duke of Anjou. Many English people are horrified because he is a Catholic. Elizabeth's predecessor, Mary Tudor, had enforced her Catholic beliefs on her subjects with hundreds of burning Protestants. A return to such inflammatory tactics is abhorrent to you and the majority of your fellow Tudors. But who will dare to tell the queen (who, as you know, is not noted for her sweet and tolerant nature)?

Puritan John Stubbs was brave enough (or stupid enough) to write a leaflet attacking Elizabeth's courtship. The punishment was to cut off the hand that wrote it. His hand is placed on the block and a blade across the wrist. A hammer is raised to strike the blade. Stubbs uses his remaining hand to wave his hat in the air and cry, 'God save the Queen' . . . before he faints. A sharp lesson to all publishers who write nasty things about the royal family.

Nominative determinism is the theory that people tend to gravitate towards areas of work that fit their names. A man called Stubbs was always going to end up with an arm cut short at the wrist.

In the end, Elizabeth I rejected the proposal of Anjou and remained unmarried. Because of objections like the Stubbs pamphlet? Or because Elizabeth was in fact a man – switched as a toddler with the Bisley Boy? But that's another story.*

SPEECHES – WASHINGTON QUOTING PAINE AT VALLEY FORGE, 1776

As a revolting person, you may sway the masses in your favour with an eloquent speech. You know the sort of thing – 'Friends, Romans, countrymen, lend me your ears,' as Mark Antony never said (not even in Latin). You can use a speech-writer to make it convincing, and your voice can add passion and clarity, as well as reaching the listeners who are unable to read.

American Independence rebel George Washington didn't have the eloquence of Shakespeare, so he used the words of the great orator Thomas Paine (1737–1809). The war had been going badly and Paine wrote a series of essays to the troops. Washington read one to his men.

---

* Briefly: in 1542 Henry VIII ignored his daughter, Princess Elizabeth, who was shuffled off to be raised in Bisley, Gloucestershire, by Thomas Parry and Lady Kat Ashley. The princess died and her guardians panicked when Henry VIII announced he would be visiting the child. They replaced the dead girl with a red-haired boy who resembled her. The pretence was sustained throughout the 'Queen's' life.

Some soldiers may have nodded off – it's a long essay – but enough were inspired to turn their fortunes around. The language is rousing: 'Tyranny, like hell, is not easily conquered; yet we have this consolation with us, that the harder the conflict, the more glorious the triumph.'

That's the carrot. The stick was to suggest you might as well fight because if you surrender you'll be slaughtered: 'It is the madness of folly to expect mercy.'

British Brits slaughtering American Brits? Unlikely. But it does no harm to demonize the enemy.

A model speech. Friends, soldiers, countrymen, fight and risk possible death; or surrender and suffer certain death. Washington's army went on to victory – and Paine's speech gets the credit.

PETITIONS – THE CHARTISTS, 1839

In the 1830s the Chartists wanted suffrage for men – but not women. Their tactic of choice was to petition for peaceful change. It was a nice idea.

There were 1.3 million signatures on the first Chartist petition to the House of Commons in July 1839. One problem was that the petition was treated as a joke by many, and signatures included

- Queen Victoria
- King Arthur
- Robin Hood
- Julius Caesar

- Bessie the Cow
- Polly the Parrot

More poignantly

- 'A Starving Man'
- 'An Unemployed Worker'
- 'The Ignored Masses'

The three-mile-long petition had no effect. The Chartists broke out into open rebellion, leading to multiple deaths. That November in Newport, Wales, several Chartists were arrested and imprisoned in the Westgate Hotel. Four thousand fellow Chartists armed themselves with makeshift weapons and marched to free them but were met by the army. Around twenty protestors were killed. The riot leaders were transported to Australia.

Enthusiasm for Chartism and its petitions made no more progress until 1842. A charismatic Irishman named Feargus O'Connor (1796–1855) became a leading light in the movement. In 1847 O'Connor was elected MP for Nottingham, just as the rest of Europe began to simmer with revolution. A new petition was to be presented to Parliament on 10 April 1848, backed by a march of tens of thousands. The meeting place was Kennington Common, which was across the river Thames from the Houses of Parliament. How did the government respond? That's right, the government simply blocked the bridges with troops and police.

The great revolt was a wash-out – literally. It wasn't just the blocked bridges that thwarted the petitioners. That march from Kennington was a failure because heavy rain kept the protestors at home. Rain stopped play at Kennington, as it would many times at the Oval cricket ground there.*

Economic prosperity, and O'Connor's descent into madness, saw the movement fade away. The mills of Parliament – like the mills of God – grind slowly. Adult men in Britain were granted universal suffrage when the Representation of the People Act was passed in 1918 – seventy years after the washed-out 1848 petition. By then the First World War had removed almost a million from the electoral register – permanently. And women would have to wait still longer.

Petitions have their value, but not when they are signed by Cleopatra.

BARRICADES – FRANCE, 1848

Barricades disrupt normal life and are harder to ignore than petitions. The French seem to have cornered the market in this rebel tactic. Even in the twenty-first century, the use of tractors to block main roads is the love-child of the revolutionary barricade . . . and the modern French authorities don't have Napoleonic grapeshot to disperse them.

---

* A lesson for all wannabe protest marchers: try and pick a sunny day.

164

In 1848 the use of barricades in Paris wasn't new but that year's revolt is remembered for them. The 1848 February Revolution began with protests against King Louis-Philippe's government. The protests turned violent after a soldier fired into a crowd. Furniture, cobblestones and carts proved effective rebel fortifications as well as symbols of the revolt. Within days King Louis-Philippe had abdicated and a new Republic had been declared.

The British farmers (of course) have a more civilized approach. In 2024, Welsh farmers placed 5,500 empty pairs of wellington boots on the steps of the Welsh Assembly building in a protest against the Welsh Government's new agricultural policy. Each pair of barricade boots symbolized a job lost due to the scheme. As barriers go, 11,000 Welsh wellies are less effective than a thousand French tractors.

Barricades succeed. The Welsh wellies are gone, and the farmers still wait for justice. Another lesson for us all.

MARCHES – MARCH ON WASHINGTON, 1963

If you want to protest for change then begin by changing your shoes, hit the roads and march. A march can be an impressive sight as you sing your protest songs and are cheered by the oppressed masses who line the roads . . . or hide in their hovels to avoid any association with your anti-authority tactics.

In the Jarrow Crusade, a peaceful march, two hundred

men took twenty-six days to reach London from the poverty-stricken town to petition Parliament in 1936. They wanted government support to reopen their shipyard. They got nothing. Optimists say they raised awareness of workers' rights, but 'awareness' doesn't put food on the table.

Some marches have ended when the protestors were met with tanks – Tiananmen Square in 1989 is the most graphic example of that. Others, unlike Jarrow, have led to real change. All you need is a quarter of million people to join you.

The 1963 March on Washington combined two protests in one – always economical. The causes were jobs and freedom. The marchers aimed to highlight the inequalities faced by African Americans a century after emancipation. As is the way of history, something spontaneous and accidental changed the dynamic for ever: Martin Luther King made his legendary 'I Have a Dream' speech.

Spontaneous and accidental, you cry. How so? King didn't plan to use the 'dream' theme until a gospel star on the platform, Mahalia Jackson, called out to him, 'Tell 'em about the dream, Martin, tell 'em about the dream,' referring to a familiar theme he had referenced in earlier speeches. And the movement had its sound bite that would travel the world: 'I have a dream that my four little children will one day live in a nation where they will not be judged by the colour of their skin but by the content of their character.'

Less than five years later King was assassinated by a petty criminal. King is gone, but his dream lives on.

REASON TO REVOLT 7
RELIGION

*'Men fear death as children fear to go into the dark
and as that natural fear in children is increased
with tales, so is the other.'*

SIR FRANCIS BACON (1561–1626) – ENGLISH ESSAYIST

Humans have found that one of the best ways to deal with a fear is to pretend it is never going to happen. Logic says death is a great abyss of nothingness? 'No, it's not,' your tribe says. 'It is a place of light and happiness where we'll meet up with those who have gone before.'

They look down on the conflicting evidence of dead Granny's body . . . cremated or buried or fed to flocks of famished pigeons. Ignore the body, they argue. 'Granny had a spirit, and that spirit has gone to an afterlife. We're pleased for her . . . and her estate will see us comfortable.'

The people in charge of this afterlife – let's call them 'gods' or 'God' – look like humans and behave like humans but with extra-ordinary powers. We can even talk to them and ask for favours, but usually they need some sort of bribe or sacrifice. Cut the throat of a goat, or maybe rip out the beating heart of a prisoner of war if you are an Aztec.

Next, you will need an earthly person to intercede on your behalf. Let's call them 'priests'. And a special place where your god is available 24/7 for a chat, though S/He may prefer 10 a.m. on a Sunday morning. Let's call that place a temple or a church, shall we? Go there often enough and you won't die, you'll just pass on to join your god in that happy place. Let's call it heaven. Sorted. We have invented 'religion'.

All of this religious stuff is fairly innocuous (unless you happen to be a sacrificial goat or an Aztec prisoner). The problems start when another tribe says they have a different god, or worship the same god in a different way, and if you don't convert they may have to kill you.

Countless millions have died in the name of religion. And as they die they realize they have one thing in common with their enemy. They all sing the same song from the same hymn sheet, and you know how it goes: 'God is on my side.'

THE TABORITE REBELS IN BOHEMIA, 1420

History casts a long shadow. In the case of the Taborites' religious wars, the shadow was cast five hundred years ahead, as far as the First World War, which it helped the Allies to win. All right, that's a little fanciful, but follow their story and make up your own mind.

In the 1400s many Bohemian people were disillusioned with the Catholic Church. It was wealthy while the people struggled to make a living, and its priests were dishonest and mostly foreigners. They were just *asking* to be rebelled against.

Jan Hus was a Catholic priest who taught at the University of Prague. Biting the papal hand that fed him, he began preaching against the Pope in 1410. Popes could forgive your sins if you paid them the going rate – a practice known as selling indulgences – so you could buy a first-class ticket into heaven.

That outraged Jan, who claimed that the Pope was not the head of the church, Jesus was, and you wouldn't catch Christ selling indulgences. Furthermore, Jan argued, a bad Pope should be sacked and replaced. The furious popes (Alexander V then John XXIII) excommunicated Hus – four times. In the end, Pope John summoned Jan to appear before a church council to explain himself at the Council of Constance.

Naturally Jan wanted a guarantee of safe conduct and was granted it. Equally naturally, his conduct was about as unsafe as you could imagine. The rebel must have suspected this because he wrote his will before he left home. Arriving at the council meeting, Jan was told to recant his views. He refused and was sentenced to be burnt at the stake for heresy.

Hus was the Czech word for 'goose', and Jan's Hus was cooked. A pun Jan himself indulged in on his way to death, when he threatened his captors: 'You may kill a weak goose, but more powerful birds, eagles and falcons, will come after me.'

Jan's followers were imaginatively named Hussites, and they took up the cause of rebellion against the papacy. The popes sent four crusades against the Bohemians, and all failed because of the superior military skills of the Hussites. King Wenceslas IV of Bohemia gave the Hussites political power, and it looked as if the rebellion against the Church had succeeded.* The ashes of Jan Hus must have been very happy.

As is the way of the world, the rebels split into factions and the most extreme Hussite faction was the Taborite. The Taborites believed the old, corrupt world would come to an end and a fresh paradise on Earth would arise. Before that could happen (we're still waiting), the weakling Wenceslas IV was bullied by his Catholic brother Sigismund into getting rid of the Hussite councillors.

Wenceslas the Wimp did as he was told (which is healthier than being chopped up at the church door). In July 1419 the Hussites were replaced by new councillors and the Taborite believers were furious. They marched into the town hall, grabbed the new councillors and threw them out of the windows – upstairs windows, naturally. A deadly defenestration.

Sigismund took up the Pope's crusades against the recalcitrant Taborite peasants, yet failed repeatedly. Knights in shining armour against peasants in shiny rags? No contest, you'd think. So how did the Hussites prevail?

When the Taborites went into battle they wanted to stay alive long enough to enjoy paradise on Earth, so they devised a weapon, five hundred years ahead of its time, to kill without

---

* Their supportive monarch was not the 'Good King Wenceslas' you'll have sung about in the Christmas carol. That 'Good' King Wenceslas was Wenceslas the First (907–35), who was chopped up at a church door by his younger brother, Boleslaus the Cruel, for spreading Christianity through his country.

getting killed. They came up with *Wagenburgs* or 'wagon-forts'. When a peasant Taborite army met a strong force of armoured knights they would circle (or square) their farm wagons then chain them together.

These wagons would be studded with iron to make them impenetrable fortresses against armoured cavalry. The crews of each wagon carried crossbows, guns, pikes and flails. The Taborite artillery carried an early form of a howitzer, and when the enemy came close the gunners would come out and inflict casualties at close range. Having battered the enemy, the second stage would begin. Taborite infantry with swords, flails, and poleaxes would emerge and attack alongside their own cavalry that had been protected in the square.

Defend from behind a fortified vehicle then emerge to counterattack? The Taborites had invented the principle of the tank.

The *Wagenburgs* were most effective on flat plains so were not copied widely down the centuries. They became obsolete when powerful cannon replaced the arrows of the attackers. Wooden wagons, like wooden warships in later years, had the fatal flaw of sending splinters into the crews.

Fast-forward five hundred years to the First World War. The invention of armour plating to deflect cannon shells, the internal combustion engine to power the counter-attack and caterpillar tracks to combat the uneven terrain. What have you got? You have a Little Willie. Or, if you'd prefer, a tank.* That was the code

---

* You can still see the original Little Willie at Bovington Tank Museum in England, the first of a long line of models that are still used with destructive force today.

name applied by the British army in the First World War and the name stuck even after they were no longer secret.

The principle of a mobile defensive shield capable of turning to attack is an echo of the followers of a roasted goose. Fittingly the Taborites believed in social and economic equality for all. Their *Wagenburgs* ensured that the grandest of knights could be defeated by the meanest of peasants. Tanks are a true symbol of levelling up.

In 1435 the Taborite fortresses were taken, and many defenders hanged in the Old Town Square of Prague. The movement was taken over by moderates. By 1452 the Taborite home of Tabor was occupied, and the rebel bid for independence came to an end. So did the promise of paradise on Earth. 'The true paradises are the paradises that we have lost,' as French novelist Marcel Proust wrote. It was a nice dream while it lasted.

POPÉ – THE PUEBLOS, 1675

There are many occasions when rebellion is understandable. In the province of Santa Fe de Nuevo México, in 1680, the indigenous people had suffered years of abuse from their Spanish occupiers. They had endured over a hundred years of Spanish armies, Spanish settlers and – worst of all – Spanish missionaries.

In 1599 the conquistador Juan de Oñate faced a rebellion by Pueblo Native Americans who had killed a dozen Spanish soldiers. He retaliated by killing up to a thousand natives. In a contest against bows and arrows the cannon usually wins. Oñate was said to have ordered that all surviving men over twenty-five have their right foot cut off – or at least a few toes, some reports say, so they remained useful as slave labour. To some, Juan de Oñate was a hero, and a statue was erected in Alcade, New Mexico.*

By 1675 the Pueblos were still resentful of the Spanish conquistadors but paid lip service to the Catholic faith. It was when the whole community came under pressure that the stress lines began to widen into cracks. A drought hit the region. Apache raids added to the trauma of hunger. The Spanish settlers were reduced to eating leather hides and straps. The native Americans turned to their old religion for comfort. That was too much for the Catholic missionaries. The pious Spanish had the traditional native masks, prayer sticks and effigies burnt. (This was a bit rich considering the Catholics worshipped an effigy of the Virgin Mary.)

Around fifty Pueblo medicine men were charged with witchcraft. Three were sentenced to death by hanging while a fourth prisoner killed himself. The remaining men were publicly whipped and sentenced to prison. The Pueblo leaders demanded the release of those prisoners. Since most of his forces were away fighting the Apache, the Spanish leader capitulated. One of the released men was Popé, who would grow in stature over the next five years.

Most revolts have a figurehead and Popé would be the symbol of the Pueblo revolt. He began plotting with the simple aim of driving out the Spanish and returning the Pueblo to their time-honoured ways. The traditional gods would end the misery of

---

* In 1998, protestors with a fine sense of irony cut off the right foot of the statue and left a note saying, 'Fair is fair.' They could have said, 'An eye for an eye, a toe for a toe.'

Apache raids and hunger; those gods would then restore prosperity to the true believers.

The strategy was to have each Pueblo settlement eliminate its own Spanish enclave of governors, priests and colonists. Hasta la vista, baby. For security there were no written messages. Two young men were given pieces of string, each with the same number of knots. The leaders of each Pueblo community would untie a knot a day. When the last one was untied the rebellion would begin. Sadly, the two young men were captured by the Spanish and tortured to reveal the secret of the knotted string. Popé brought the rebellion forward by a day. Hundreds of Spanish died in the rebellion, including twenty-one of the thirty-three Franciscan missionaries, who went to meet their own god earlier than they had probably planned. Churches were destroyed and the surviving Spanish settlers fled.

Popé had promised a Pueblo paradise. The ancient gods disappointed as gods are wont to do; neither the famine nor the Apache raiders went away, no matter how much they prayed. Inevitably Popé was deposed within a year of the revolt and disappeared from the pages of history to some unknown fate.

In time many of the desperate native communities invited the Spanish to return in peace. Within ten years the Spanish were back in control – and yet the fight had not been in vain. The Spanish made land grants to the Pueblo people, giving them a legal advocate to represent the natives in Spanish courts. Above all, they never again tried to impose Catholicism on the people. Mass was replaced by masks, prayer books by prayer sticks and saintly statues by effigies.

Not all revolts end in total defeat. Still, had that compromise been reached seventy-five years earlier, a lot of lives and toes would have been saved.

YAA ASANTEWAA – ASHANTI WAR OF THE GOLDEN STOOL, 1900

It does help to have God on your side. However, if God has thoughtfully armed you with machine guns against the bows and spears of the opposition then it is only right and proper of you to impose your god on the indigenous people. That was the thinking behind the invasion of other lands in the name of the British Empire.

The Asante (Ashanti) people fought against the British intruders in five wars between 1824 and 1900. They were located in the area we now call south-west Ghana and had a thriving trade in slaves. They were known to start wars in the region with the main purpose of collecting their victims. Each warrior carried a knife for removing the head of anyone who resisted. By the 1820s, the British interlopers were trying to impose a ban on slaving and, as you may imagine, this was not popular. King Osei Bonsu of the Ashanti expressed the opinion that a ban on slavery was a bit rich coming from the Brits, given their former eager involvement in the trade.

The legendary King Osei Tutu had united the small local tribes into the Asante nation and his leading priest gave the new people a symbol that they could unite behind: a stool. Not just any old stool but a golden stool that Asante kings would be crowned on.* The stool was said to have descended from the sky and landed at

---

* Like the Scottish Stone of Scone that the English nicked to place under the coronation throne, it had a ceremonial, mystic purpose.

the feet of Osei Tutu during one of their religious ceremonies. Okomfo Anokye, the head priest, claimed that it contained all the spirits of the deceased Asante, and it drove his people on to even greater territorial gains and conquests. The fact that Osei Tutu traded slaves for guns with the British and Dutch probably helped trounce the opposition as effectively as the stool. The main thing is, the Asante revered it.

The Brits were able to enforce their ban because they controlled the Ghana coast. The Asante with their head-chopping habit were tough, but the country's wealth of ivory and gold still made it worth a little pain for the gain. However, in a battle at Nsamankow in 1824 the under-equipped British forces were caught off guard. The British governor Sir Charles MacCarthy was either killed or killed himself to avoid capture. The result was the same: the Asante removed his noble head. It was such a rare trophy that they fashioned the skull into a drinking cup for their king to use on ceremonial occasions.

It's fair to say that British/Asante relations never recovered. In the next seven decades, four more wars broke out and the Asante tactics were cruel but imaginative . . .

- They would cut telegraph wires between forts, so the British outposts were cut off from the cities.
- The Brits had to use messengers to carry letters.
- These messengers would be captured and hung by the ankles.
- Then the telegraph wire would be used to whip their feet till they bled.
- The messengers were then set free to carry the messages . . . if they could.

The trade squabbles were nasty, but the worst conflict erupted in 1900 because of that holy golden stool (which, as you'll remember, contained the ghosts of all the predeceased Asante). It was buried at the king's palace till it was needed for a royal ceremony. There was one strict rule about the beatific bum-rest – a sort of golden rule: nobody sits on it except the king. That may be a quirky little rule for the ruler but let's face it, you wouldn't want some stranger's bottom parked on the spirit of your beloved ancestor, would you?

British governor Fred Hodgson was too stupid and arrogant to understand this. In March 1900 he marched into the Ashanti capital and demanded the stool. He told the defenders that the king no longer ruled – they were now the subjects of Queen Victoria. As their ruler she must be given the stool. Fatuous Fred was so arrogant and stupid, he said that as Queen Vic's representative he must be allowed to sit on the stool himself. You can hear the rising pitch of his pipsqueak voice as he told the assembled Asante: 'Where is the Golden Stool? I am the representative of the Paramount Power. Why have you downgraded me to this ordinary chair? Why did you not take the opportunity of my visit to bring the Golden Stool for me to sit upon?'

The speech was met with a silence as great as Lewis Carroll's oysters': answer came there none.

Fred was deluded because he seemed to believe, as recorded in *Hansard* in 1901, that 'if he could only get possession of the Golden Stool he would be able to govern the country for all time'. Statesman David Lloyd George explained to Parliament, 'Frederick Hodgson's quest of the Golden Stool was something like the quest of the Holy Grail.' He rather failed to appreciate the symbolic importance of another nation's holy symbols.

The silent chiefs were voluble among themselves when they discussed their response. It had to be war. Those who hung back were berated by the queen mother of the Asante (and legend in modern-day Ghana), Yaa Asantewaa. This was her battle-cry:

> I must say this, If you the men of the Asante will not go forward, we the women will fight. We will fight till the last of us falls on the battlefield. We will fight till the last of us falls in the fields and forests. We will fight till the last of us falls in the streets. I shall fight till the very end.

Winston Churchill must have read that speech before he echoed it in the Second World War. Though unlike Churchill, Yaa Asantewaa really did lead her warriors into battle.

Between Fred's self-important ego and Yaa Asantewaa's rousing speech a bloody war started. If the Asante were brave warriors then the British God gave his people the fire-power which they gloated over. One officer James Willcocks reported, 'When a good number of Asante had come out into the open, 7-pounders and Maxims were turned on them with excellent effect.'

'Excellent effect' indeed. Not courage but mechanical force. Governor Fred Hodgson escaped (and would go on blundering across the empire, tactlessly upsetting other native peoples for some time). A thousand British died in the needless Yaa Asantewaa war. But the Asante fared far worse. As David Lloyd George put it so graphically to Parliament, 'The foolish policy in regard to the Golden Stool, had led to the hundreds and thousands of the corpses of savages festering.'

Yaa Asantewaa was arrested and exiled to the Seychelles, where she died four thousand miles from home.

And the Golden Stool? You'll want to know its fate. It had been hidden in the Asante forests and was stumbled upon by a group of native workers. They nicked the gold ornaments and left the wood (even though it had been brought to Earth from heaven). The thieves were sentenced to death for this blasphemous act, but pardoned by the British.

Hundreds and thousands of corpses in a forgotten war, and all because Hopeless Hodgson wanted to sit on a stool. But that is the nature of religious wars. For God's sake . . .

FACE YOUR PUNISHMENT

'A nation of slaves is always prepared to applaud the clemency of their master who, in the abuse of absolute power, does not proceed to the last extremes of injustice and oppression.'

EDWARD GIBBON (1737–94) – ENGLISH HISTORIAN

Rebellion is inevitably against the ruling class. Those ruling classes make the laws and attach punishments for those who breach them. The law says, 'Don't exceed 30 miles per hour along this stretch of road' and you're caught doing 31mph? Face a fine or be forcibly retrained to mend your rebellious ways. While you moan at the inconvenience, the victims of speeding drivers (and the victims' families) will be cheering.

The Genevan philosopher Jean-Jacques Rousseau (1712–78) would point out that in return for obeying the laws we are protected by them. So, the Boy Scout who is helping the frail old lady across the road should be protected from your reckless driving. That will be pointed out to you when you attend your humiliating 'speed awareness course'.

What won't be pointed out to you is how lucky you are not to have broken some of the historic laws. Draco was an Athenian legislator in ancient Greece around the seventh century BC. He is remembered for creating a written legal code for Athens, replacing the previous unwritten laws and blood feuds. He is notorious for the severity of those laws. Steal vegetables? You risk execution. Owe money? Face being enslaved. The punishments were, well, draconian. Incidentally Draco was very popular in ancient Athens. Too popular, according to one legend. The lawmaker died in the Aegina theatre when, in a shower of adoration, his supporters supposedly threw so many hats and cloaks at him that he suffocated.

Many past lawmakers didn't want to punish, of course. They wanted to deter. Who were these lawgivers and what were their rules? Glad you asked.

BURNING AT THE STAKE, 1553-8

Not every vicious execution is an act of terror designed to have people living in fear.

Henry VIII's daughter Mary was a Catholic. When she came to the throne in 1553 she obliged everyone to return to her version of the faith. Those who rebelled against her and retained their Protestant practices would be punished, often by burning at the stake. Mary ordered 274 men, women and children to die this way.

Kind Mary believed that fire would burn away all evil so their purified souls could then go straight to heaven.

She was doing the victims a favour by burning them. Her authority came from the Bible, which said, 'The angels shall gather all things that offend and shall cast them into a furnace of fire.' Does that make them hell's angels?

To spare the victims' suffering they often had pouches of gunpowder strapped to their legs and arms. Instead of a slow sizzle there was just a quick bang, and bits were blown to heaven before they knew it. Others would be strangled beforehand, so they didn't suffer slow agony.

Neither system was infallible. Sometimes the fires started so quickly the executioner couldn't climb up the stake in time to effect the strangulation. Other times, the damp wood burnt so slowly the gunpowder wasn't ignited. No fire escape for those poor souls.

HANGING – THE RIOT ACT, 1715

What can the forces of law do when people gather to riot? Nowadays they apply the Public Order Act and dispersal orders, but for 250 years they read the Riot Act of 1715:

> Our sovereign lord the King chargeth and
> commandeth all persons, being assembled,
> immediately to disperse themselves, and peaceably to
> depart to their habitations, or to their lawful business,
> upon the pains contained in the act made in the first

year of King George, for preventing tumults and riotous assemblies. God save the King.

It came about because of the Sacheverell riots of 1710, the Coronation Riots of 1714 and the 1715 riots. In the first of these, a staunch Anglican clergyman called Henry Sacheverell read sermons that claimed there were two threats to Britain – the Catholics and the Dissenters (Protestants who had separated from the Church of England). From his pulpit he ranted at the Catholics for a full, dull three minutes. But don't head for the exit just yet. He spoke against the Dissenters for another hour and a half. He sold a hundred thousand copies of his sermon and his supporters set off to burn down a Presbyterian meeting house in Lincoln's Inn Fields.

Sacheverell was banned from preaching so, of course, he became a martyr. Riots spread across the country. His sermons were burnt in public. That many copies of an hour-and-three-quarter speech must have made a good bonfire.

But it wasn't just Dissenters the rioters objected to. Many of them were opposed to the influx of ten thousand Calvinist refugees from Germany who came to Britain. They wanted a tougher immigration policy and border controls to keep the foreigners of a different belief out of Britain. (Differing religions and unwelcome immigrants – sound familiar?)

Imagine the rioters' fury when Queen Anne died, and German George I came to the throne in 1714.

Coming over here, taking our crown. Sacheverell was
in the West Country and it's no coincidence that this
was where the Coronation Riots flared up. Were you
having a street party for the coronation? Sacheverell's
supporters would attack you. Want your local vicar to
ring the church bells in celebration? The Sacheverell
devotees won't – in fact in Newton Abbot he's removed
the clappers so you can't.

In Cornwall there were more risings in support of
the Scottish Jacobites. This was a fiercely loyal Anglican
population who were struggling with high taxes and
unemployment . . . unemployment exacerbated by foreign
workers taking many of the mining jobs. The German
Georges were always going to be as welcome as a fox in a
henhouse. The Cornish answer? Bring back the Stuarts . . .
or anyone except those German Georges. They seemed to
overlook the fact the Stuarts were followers of the detested
Catholic religion . . . just not quite so detested as the
Dissenters.

In the face of this challenge to its authority, the
government felt it needed stronger law enforcement, and
so it introduced the Riot Act. Protestors in the Sacheverell
riots and the Coronation Riots had been fined, jailed or
whipped in public afterwards. But the new Riot Act said
that if they didn't disperse within an hour they could be
forced to go . . . and soldiers using force were exempt from
punishment if they happened to kill or maim a rioter. In
an extreme case, ignoring the reading of the Riot Act could
get you hanged.

Hanged? For protesting? It's hard to feel sympathy for rioting bigots who have religious and racial prejudices. But hanging? Riot or wrong?

PITCH-CAPPING - UNITED IRISHMEN REVOLT, 1798

A punishment that involves an agonizing death may be seen as an even greater deterrent than a quick execution as envisaged by the kindly Joseph-Ignace Guillotin.

The grotesque psychopath Henry VIII heard that the Bishop of Rochester's cook had poisoned a meal before serving it to the bishop's guests and was sentenced to hang. Henry decided that hanging was too good for the man. He said he wanted the cook boiled alive in his own pot. When his legal advisers said that the law did not allow boiling alive, the king said, 'Change the law'. They did, and for the rest of Henry's reign the punishment for poisoning was to be boiled alive.

It sounds barbaric but other torturous punishments were inflicted well into the 'modern' age. Punishments like 'pitch-capping'. This involved placing a conical paper cap onto the victim's head. Hot pitch or tar was poured into the cap and it would harden as it cooled, sticking to the scalp. When it was ripped off it would take hair, skin and flesh with it. The scarring was permanent and, although it was not the intention, death could result from infection.

Medieval? No, it was used by the British against the 1798 Irish rebels as well as some of their supporters. The aim was not simply to extract information from the rebels but also to intimidate the rest of the population.

DEATH BY ELEPHANT – SRI LANKA, 1795

If you are an advocate of a non-violent society then how do you defend yourself when a violent one descends upon you? In the 1700s the island of Sri Lanka was full of rich temples and peaceful people – the Singhalese. Then the Portuguese arrived and started stealing their gold and their spices, their jewels and their women. The native people needed to defend themselves but didn't have European guns. However, they were good at concealing themselves in forests, and setting traps and ambushes. A Portuguese gun isn't worth the metal it's forged from when a Singhalese guerrilla drops a boulder on your head as you walk under a cliff.

As a Portuguese occupier you didn't want to become isolated in those forests and captured. Fifty Portuguese prisoners were sent back to their barracks with ten eyes between them – and they'd all had their naughty bits cut off too. That's what I'd call a deterrent.

By the time the Brits arrived in 1795 the Singhalese had some tasty tricks up their sleeves. The indigenous people were Buddhists, so they were not so keen on taking the lives of their British enemies. At the same time, they wanted to eliminate the invaders. An easily solved conundrum: captive Brits could simply be laid out on the ground, and if a specially trained elephant should trample on them, that wasn't technically breaking the rules.

TRANSPORTATION - THE TOLPUDDLE MARTYRS, 1833

As the Georgian era came to a close, the judges devised an evil alternative to the gallows for the two hundred capital offences on the law books. They could send the criminals to Australia. Rid Britain of the dregs and save on rope.

> God is our guide! from field, from wave,
> From plough, from anvil, and from loom;
> We come, our country's rights to save,
> And speak a tyrant faction's doom:
> We raise the watch-word liberty;
> We will, we will, we will be free.

Thus spake George Loveless, a member of the Tolpuddle society.

In the 1830s, agricultural labourers' wages were falling again. They had already been reduced to seven shillings a week and now the landowners were looking to trim them to six shillings. The labourers of Tolpuddle in Dorset said they'd not work for less than ten shillings. They formed a mutual help society – effectively a trades union.

The initiation into the society seems an echo of the entry into Freemasonry: the image of a skeleton was painted on a board; the new entrant would be blindfolded and invited to swear an oath; the blindfold was removed, and the painting given to him as a reminder of human frailty (and, of course, a menacing hint as to what would happen to traitors).

A furious local landowner/magistrate wrote to the home secretary, Lord Melbourne, demanding these Tolpuddle rebels be punished. Melbourne replied that, regrettably, existing laws against such societies had been revoked. But . . . the egregious ermine-wearer came up with a cunning alternative. He suggested the six leaders be charged under the old and unused Unlawful Oaths Act of 1797. That skeleton initiation ceremony would fit the bill nicely. They were arrested, tried and duly found guilty. The sentence was transportation to Australia for seven years.

The sentence caused outrage among workers. A massive demonstration marched through London and an 800,000-strong petition was delivered to Parliament. After three years, the government (and a new home secretary) relented, and the Tolpuddle society members returned home with free pardons and as heroes.

Not many people become 'martyrs' without dying, but transportation was no picnic in the Australian sun. The six men lost three years of their lives and suffered a lot of distress. James Brine (1813–1902) wrote afterwards about the hardships he endured. In Australia he was quickly robbed of all the bedding, clothes and (most importantly) the shoes allotted to him by the penal supervisors . . .

> I was employed to dig post-holes . . . having walked so far without shoes, my feet were so cut and sore I could not put them to the spade. I got a piece of an iron hoop and wrapped [it] round my foot to tread upon, and for six months . . . I went without shoes, clothes, or bedding, and lay on the bare ground at night. Shortly afterwards I was sent to the pool to wash sheep, and for seventeen days was working up to my breast in water. I thus caught a severe cold and having told my master that I was very ill, asked him if he would be so good as to give me something to cover me at night, if it were only a piece of horse-cloth.

That master had believed the fake news that preceded the arrival of the Tolpuddle men: troublemakers all. Brine explained:

> 'No,' said he, 'I will give you nothing until you are due for it. What would your masters in England have had to cover them if you had not been sent here? I understand it was your intention to have murdered, burnt, and destroyed everything before you, and you are sent over here to be severely punished, and no mercy shall be shown you.'

Murder and destruction were not on the Tolpuddle agenda. They simply wanted ten shillings a week.

The working-class martyrs of Tolpuddle may have returned to Britain as national heroes, but the Dorset landowners still saw them as a threat to their wealth and comfort. They forced five of the six returning convicts to seek new lives in Canada, where they settled as farmers in London, Ontario.

James Hammett alone returned to Tolpuddle. How did the country treat this hero of the working classes? Hammett died in the Dorchester workhouse in 1891. A bit of a clue there as to the answer.

REASON TO REVOLT 8

FREEDOM

'Man will never be free until the last king is strangled with the entrails of the last priest.'

DENIS DIDEROT (1713–84) – FRENCH PHILOSOPHER

The French philosopher Denis Diderot was buried at Saint-Denis Basilica among French royalty, which is a little odd given his recommendation that they all be throttled. Within ten years of his death, the French Revolution had turned the people against the royals, so the Basilica was desecrated, the corpses dug up and scattered. In a laudable nod to recycling, the lead coffins were melted down for reuse and the corpses dumped in a mass grave. Many bodies, Diderot's included, would have been dismembered. Rest in pieces.

OWAIN GLYNDŴR – WELSH NATIONAL LEADER, 1400

It can be useful to have someone with social status leading a rebellion. They are used to telling people what to do, for one thing. Owain Glyndŵr (1354–1415) was definitely in the gentle-man class. He was one of the wealthiest of the Welsh squires. Along with his Welsh compatriots he became increasingly irri-tated that the English laws were prejudicial to the Welsh. He was in dispute with a neighbour across the border and the legal system seemed weighted in favour of the English lord.

Although Owain was posh, his discontent was typical of the Welsh of all classes. The Welsh were ready to revolt but the fuse was lit by a superstition: local prophets announced that the world was coming to an end in the year 1400. The peasants were determined to make the most of the time they had left, and they elected Owain Glyndŵr as their leader – a role he readily adopted.

English attempts to crush the revolt were initially ham-pered by terrible weather. The rebels claimed God was on their side, though cynics would point out that Wales and rain are no strangers. Owain Glyndŵr was seen as a saviour and was happy to adopt the mantle. He said, 'I promise to deliver my fellow countrymen from the oppression and the captivity they have suffered since the days of Cadwaladr. I have been chosen, by God, to release the Welsh from the slavery of our English enemies.'

The Welsh were not slaves but a bit of economy with the truth never hurt a rebel leader. Glyndŵr's forces won battle after battle until the English king Henry IV's son proved to be a greater general than his father. He was, of course the future Henry V, whose martial prowess at Agincourt in 1415 was celebrated by Will Shakespeare.

The Bard put the famous words into Henry V's mouth . . .

Once more unto the breach, dear friends, once more;
Or close the wall up with our English dead.

That second line is written in perfect iambic pentameter and that would be ruined if Shakespeare had aimed for historical accuracy and written: 'Or close the wall up with our English and Welsh dead'. Around five hundred Welsh archers contributed to Henry's contingent of six to seven thousand archers at Agincourt.*

Ironically, in 1405 Henry junior was Prince of Wales, the country he was about to lay waste to. He inflicted heavy casualties on the Welsh army, including the abbot of Llantarnam, who was caring for the wounded, at a battle near Usk, and the Welsh revolt turned against Owain Glyndŵr. Owain's younger brother, Tudor, was hacked to death and three hundred Welsh soldiers were beheaded by the English near the river Usk which was a bit of a downer. By 1408 Owain had lost Aberystwyth Castle. In 1409 the English took Harlech and captured Owain's family, but not Owain, who slipped away to the mountains to continue the fight. He disappeared, probably dying at his sister's house in 1415.

The rebellion failed and the Welsh were as badly off as ever. The squires of Wales tried to disown Owain Glyndŵr. They said he was a crazy rebel – nothing to do with them. But the poor never forgot him.

Later, in the 1700s, the antiquarian Thomas Pennant collected

---

* The Welsh archers were not the key to Henry V's victory at Agincourt as the persistent myth says, but they did contribute, so we have to conclude that Owain Glyndŵr was forgiven and quickly forgotten by the English.

the stories of Owain that restored him as the chief hero of the Welsh. He's still alive, you know. Sitting in a cave playing chess with King Arthur. Waiting for the day when the Welsh need a hero to save them. But perhaps you wouldn't want to be saved by such a ruthless warlord. For instance, there was the time Owain Glyndŵr took Radnor Castle. Sixty of the garrison surrendered and were disarmed. They threw themselves on Owain's mercy. He ordered that they be killed, which was not what they had in mind.

Glyndŵr's men devastated the towns they defeated. These were still feeling the effects 120 years later. In Tudor times Sir John Wynn wrote, 'I visited the towns of Hay and Radnor and they still bore the scars of Glyndŵr's revolt. Green grass grew on the market-place in Llanrwst and the deer fed in the churchyard.'

Owain was apparently ruthless even to his own family. Four hundred years after his death an old oak tree near Dolgellau was being shown to Victorian visitors and they were told that Owain met his cousin Hywel near there to sort out an argument they'd had. The cousin was a friend of the English and, when they met, cousin Hywel tried to kill Owain. But Owain was prepared. He was wearing armour under his clothes. Owain killed Hywel. Then he burnt his house to the ground. After that he refused to give his cousin a Christian burial. Instead, he brought the corpse to the oak and stuffed it in a hollow. The rotted corpse was found years later – just cinders and ashes. Or was that just a Victorian invention?

In 1402 there was a battle at the river Lugg. The Welsh had attacked Radnorshire and English nobleman Edmund Mortimer raised an army of tenants and supporters to meet the threat. Mortimer's men had to climb a hill to meet Glyndŵr's. Add to that the fact many of his tenants were Welsh and defected to the other side and he had no chance. The Welsh tenants simply turned around and fired at their English brothers-in-arms. The English were slaughtered – but Mortimer's Welsh soldiers? They just said, 'Hello, lads, nice to see you. We weren't really fighting for Mortimer. We just came along so we could meet up with you and join Glyndŵr's army.' Shakespeare remembered that little battle in his *Henry IV Part One*:

The noble Mortimer,
Leading the men of Herefordshire to fight,
Against the wild and irregular Glendower,
Was by the rude hand of that Welshman taken,
A thousand of his people butchered

Not just the rude hands of Welshmen. But even ruder hands of Welsh women. (Those of a delicate disposition may like to skip to the next section.) The Welsh were accompanied by women camp-followers who entered the battlefield to loot the English corpses. Reports say they took especial delight in pulling down the breeches of the dead enemy, cutting off their private parts and stuffing them in the corpse's mouth. Shakespeare doesn't mention that bit.

Mortimer was captured but didn't lose any vital body parts. That was quite fortuitous as he would need them. When the English government dragged its feet over his ransom, Mortimer defected to Glyndŵr and married the Welsh leader's daughter, Catrin. He would die in the siege of Harlech Castle, while Catrin was locked in the Tower of London along with their daughters.

No happy ending for anyone, from the common soldiers to the lordly leaders.

Revolts for freedom are not all peasants' revolts.

PAVEL PESTEL AND THE DECEMBRISTS AGAINST SERFDOM, 1825

'Slave' has been such an ugly name Peter the Great (r. 1682–1725) legally abolished it in Russia in 1723. But don't strum your balalaikas in joyous celebration just yet. Peter renamed the Russian slaves as 'serfs'. They were technically not exactly the same thing as chattel slaves, since they could not be sold independently and were tied to a particular bit of land owned by the nobles. But they weren't allowed to leave and they could be forced to work, so they weren't exactly free.

Catherine the Great (r. 1762–1796) oversaw serfdom expanding into territories like Ukraine. Over time the serfs' conditions worsened as landowners acquired the same powers as slaveowners, of inflicting corporal punishment and the right to sell a serf. By the 1820s, serfs were practically indistinguishable from slaves. What's in a name?

And as the Industrial Revolution enriched the west of Europe, Russia lagged behind because of serfdom. Meanwhile, the French Revolution that had inspired slave revolts in Haiti, also stirred Russian army officers into a bid for social reform on behalf of the subjugated people. The humanitarian officers had seen their peasant soldiers suffering during the wars against Napoleon. They were motivated by the need to modernize Russia as well as a humanitarian desire to improve the lot of the serfs.

They formed the Union of Salvation – a sort of Salvation Army minus the tambourines.

In 1816 the cavalry officer and war hero Pavel Pestel (1793–1826) joined the Union of Salvation with revolutionary ideals. Emancipation was top of Pestel's reform agenda. He said:

> The benefits of giving freedom to the serfs was considered from the start. The nobility was to be invited to petition the Tsar about it, but we soon came to realise that the nobility could not be converted. When the Ukrainian nobility totally rejected a similar liberation project of their governor we knew persuasion was not going to work.

If words don't work then rebellion might, the officers decided. When a new tsar, Nicholas I, came to the Russian throne, the followers of the Union of Salvation mutinied and confronted the rest of the army who were loyal to the tsar. One of Nicholas I's generals crossed to parley with the mutineers. They surrounded him and negotiated with a bullet to the back of the general, who fell from his horse. The shooting was followed by a stabbing with a bayonet as he lay on the ground. The action on 14 December 1825 became known as the Decembrist Revolt, and it was short-lived.

Nicholas saw that the rebels were not up for a polite chat, so he sent in his cavalry to charge. This was in the central square of St Petersburg in midwinter. The horses slid and skidded on the cobbles and the scene was not so much a disaster as a farce. Nicholas then took a leaf from old enemy Napoleon's book and ordered his cannon to fire at the mutineers.

The nasty part was that he had the cannon loaded with grape-shot. This antipersonnel weapon consisted of a cloth bag filled with dozens of small iron or lead balls resembling a cluster of grapes. When fired, the cloth bag disintegrates, and the balls spread out, inflicting devastating casualties at short range. They break bones, tear the flesh and penetrate to cause internal bleeding. The real impact is to cause panic and chaos in the opposition.*

The Decembrists may have been military officers, but their tactical nous was lacking. Having run from St Petersburg Square they regrouped on the frozen river Neva to the north. No grapeshot required by the pursuing loyalist troops; ordinary cannonballs smashed the ice, and the rebels sank into the chilly river. An early example of a cold war.

Pestel had not been present at the disastrous revolt, having been arrested the day before on suspicion of a plot to assassinate the tsar. He and several other lucky leaders were hanged. The unlucky ones were exiled to Siberia. Like Toussaint Louverture in Haiti, they didn't live to see their dreams become reality.

The Decembrists' revolt is now seen as a major event in Russian history. Pestel's idealistic bid for reform and opposition to serfdom inspired successive generations of revolutionaries. Oddly, it was the argument for modernization that succeeded where humanitarian concern had failed to provoke a change.

---

* As a young Revolutionary officer, Napoleon was faced by a crowd who supported the royals in Paris on 5 October 1795. He had no compunction in ordering grapeshot to be used to disperse the mob. The action is remembered as '13 Vendémiaire' and Napoleon's ruthless order as 'a whiff of grapeshot'. Despite its barbarity, it did Napoleon's promotion prospects no harm.

The Crimean War in the 1850s brought victory for the industrialized West. Britain may have lost the Charge of the Light Brigade – with old technology – but ultimately they won with their modern weaponry. Russia realized it was simply too economically backward to survive the nineteenth century. In 1861 Tsar Alexander II finally emancipated the serfs. Pavel Pestel had not died in vain.

But maybe Peter the Great had died in vain with his slave/serf name game. Like the French revolutionaries, centuries of oppression left the peasants with a festering resentment. As the Roman historian Tacitus observed, 'A desire to resist oppression is implanted in the nature of man.' He could have added that the longer it goes on, the stronger the forces of resistance grow.

In Russia, the centuries of slavery then serfdom ensured that resentment outlasted these reforms. Revolution, when it came in 1917, led to the extermination of the aristocracy in a way that never happened under less oppressive regimes in (say) Britain. Britain had a policy of bending so it didn't break.

HŌNE HEKE POKAI – MĀORI REVOLT, 1844

Owain Glyndŵr brought a lot of pain and grief to his enemies but ultimately he failed. If he had held some of the mighty English castles in Wales then he may have fared better and lasted longer.

Castles are useful military headquarters and bases for operations. But just as importantly, they are symbols of the oppressors. Take them and you are striking a symbolic blow for your freedom fight. But symbols of oppression can take many and varied forms. They can be as small as King John's wax seal on Magna Carta or as innocuous as a piece of coloured cloth: a flag.

Knock the flag off a sailing ship in battle and the crew are demoralized. Capture a flag in a medieval battle and your army has a huge psychological boost. Not that it worked for Richard III. He rode down Bosworth Hill and made a beeline for Sir William Brandon who was carrying Henry Tudor's flag. Brandon was killed by Richard and lost the flag. It looked for a while as though the king would win, but Richard was unhorsed and lost his life.

Many conquerors display their triumph by raising their own flag and to this day rebels show their hatred of the opposition by burning the enemy flag. But to some rebels just capturing the flag is a victory.

Lieutenant-Governor William Hobson declared British sovereignty over New Zealand in 1840 after signing the Treaty of Waitangi with around forty Māori chiefs. Copies were circulated around the land and a further five hundred added their names, including at least thirteen women. The Brits gave the Māori booze and guns – the Māori gave the Brits New Zealand. Fair exchange and all that.

The first chief to sign the treaty had been Hōne Heke. In a salutary lesson to us all, he failed to read the small print which, in any event, had been tweaked in the Māori translation to make it sound a better deal than it was. It wasn't a Brit/Māori power-share. The Crown – the one on Queen Vic's head – had precedence.

Hōne Heke became disillusioned. American traders were stirring trouble and supplying weapons to Māori tribes. They told

Hōne Heke how they'd overthrown the British in the American War of Independence, so why couldn't the Māori do the same?

Hōne Heke raided the town of Kororāreka allegedly to rescue a Māori woman who was living with the local British butcher. It was really an excuse to attack. The girl had never liked Hōne Heke and didn't want to be 'rescued' – her name for him was 'Pig-head' – but during the raid a friend of Hōne Heke chopped down the flagpole with the Union Jack. And that inspired Hōne Heke.

Hōne Heke couldn't attack the British tribal chief Queen Victoria, but he could attack the sign of her power – the British Union Jack flag that flew from Flagstaff Hill (Maiki Hill) in Kororāreka (now Russell). Of course, the British erected it again so Hōne Heke chopped it down again . . . and again. Three times the flagstaff had fallen, and it was becoming a boring sort of war. British commander Captain Fitzroy tried to thwart the Māori rebels by erecting a ship's mast, thick as a tree trunk, clad in iron, then placing a large force to guard it. A challenge to the rebels. A red flag to a bull . . . or a red, white and blue flag to be accurate.

This time, six hundred armed warriors attacked the guard post and killed all the defenders. The silly game was getting serious. They moved on to attack the town. The biggest disaster was at the gunpowder magazine, where the town's supply exploded spectacularly. A Māori triumph? No. A workman had set it off with a careless spark from his pipe. More proof, if it is needed, that smoking is bad for your health.

The British defenders retreated to a warship in the bay which bombarded the rebels with cannon. Six Brits went back to collect valuables. They were hacked down.

The end was predictable, because Hōne Heke did not have the support of all the native tribes. The Brits sent in a heavily armed force to get revenge. The band played 'Rule Britannia' as they landed. The British soldiers had the help of the friendly Māori plus some *pākehā*, non-native men who had gone to live with the indigenous people. Men like Jacky Marmon, an ex-convict, who said he was so integrated with the Māori he had killed rival Māori in battle and eaten them at cannibal feasts.*

The crafty Brits attacked Hōne Heke when he left his fortress to gather food. He was badly wounded with a shot to the thigh and his key lieutenant was killed. Morale dropped but still he refused to surrender.

But Hōne Heke continued to provoke the British and even sent them a 'Brits go home' message:

> God made this country for us. It cannot be sliced. Return
> to your own country, which was made by God for you. God
> made this land for us; it is not for any stranger or foreign
> nation to meddle with this sacred country.

He was beating his head against an iron-clad flagpole by that stage.

The Brits finally defeated Heke by luck. By this time, the Māori had become Christians and thought Sunday was a day

---

* Jacky could have been lying about nibbling on natives. But Captain
  Cook had recorded that cannibalism had been practised by the
  people he came across. Naturally Cook was a biased chronicler, and
  his stories may be taken with a pinch of fava beans.

of peace. The Brits (who were also supposed to be Christians) attacked the Māori fortress at Ruapekapeka on a Sunday when the Māori were praying. (Which was a bit of a cheat. A bit like stabbing a Roman emperor when he's taking a pee.) The Brits claimed victory – most think it was a draw.

The Brits could see they were never going to win the war so they eventually offered the Māori generous terms for peace ... these terms included pardoning the indigenous fighters but called them 'rebels'. Hōne Heke and his fellow chieftains made peace once he'd been convinced that the British would stick to the treaty.

Heke died of a disease in 1850, six years after he started flattening flagpoles – but while he lived, that flagpole was never raised again. So, who won? No one. Who lost? As usual, everyone. Having said that, you can claim a small victory in that you now know to always read the small print.

LESSONS FROM HISTORY 8

FIGHT FOR THE CAUSE

'A revolution is an idea which has found its bayonets.'

NAPOLEON BONAPARTE (1769–1821) — FRENCH
LEADER

It's a fair bet that most revolting people could cite a 'cause'
for their actions. It would probably be something to elicit
your sympathy. Maybe something selfless and honourable.
'Power to the people', rather than, 'If I get to be king, I'll be
richer than if I'd won the lottery'.

It is useful to have a reason to revolt, a 'cause' to fight and
risk death for . . . someone else's death, preferably. Please
note that cutting off a monarch's head and taking power
for yourself is historically proven to offer very short-term
gain. By executing your rulers, you are making execution
acceptable, which you may not enjoy when it gets to your
turn.

ABOLITION OF PRIVILEGE – MAXIMILIEN ROBESPIERRE, 1794

If you show no mercy then you'll receive none. And that applied to French lawyer and politician Maximilien Robespierre who rose (temporarily) to the top piece of dung on the heap. His 'cause' was a society in which 'privilege' for the aristocracy and church was abolished. He also argued for incorruptibility among both the ruling class and the ruled. People who expect that in any society are naive or delusional.

It is often forgotten that Robespierre argued not for a republic, but for a constitutional monarchy in which a king would be constrained by the power of the people. In time he became more radical and instituted the infamous Reign of Terror. The lesson from this era is that violence becomes normalized and the answer to most problems. He headed the 'Department of Public Safety' (nice touch that) to eliminate enemies of the state. It soon evolved to eliminate enemies of Robespierre. When Robespierre became the problem, a member of the Parisian National Guard called Charles-André Merda (1770–1812) took a leading role in the farce.

Merda's version said he shot Robespierre and shattered his jaw. (He was promoted on the strength of his boast.) In an alternative reality it was said Robespierre knew the game was up and attempted to shoot himself through the head. Merda was a bit of a liar, but this part of his story was probably close to the truth. Robespierre had been about to sign the order that would set the army loose on the people of Paris. The paper has 'Ro . . .' at the bottom and splashes of blood on it, so it has all the hallmarks of a cold-blooded Merda.

Robespierre and his pals had sent hundreds to their deaths. Now it was their blood-soaked turn. His brother, Augustin, tried to escape by jumping from a window. He broke his leg and was caught. The third of their group, Le Bas, shot himself. The fourth, Couthon, fell down a flight of stairs in his attempt to evade arrest and gashed his forehead. A bandage was slapped on so he could live to feel the guillotine's tickle on the neck. The fifth, Hanriot, was thrown from a window – but fell on a rubbish heap and survived. Soldiers found him and tore out one eye, which was left hanging down his cheek. As he climbed onto the guillotine the following evening a spectator snatched the eye off as a souvenir.

Robespierre was patched up enough to be carried to the guillotine. The executioner tore off the bandage and his jaw almost fell away. A witness said, 'He let out a groan like a dying tiger. Everyone in the square heard it.' It didn't hurt for long. A woman screamed at Robespierre: 'Go to your grave with the curses of the wives and mothers of France. Your death makes me drunk with happiness.'

He would be mourned only by Charles-Henri Sanson, high executioner of the First French Republic in his blood-red coat.

As usual, the greatest suffering was experienced by the peasants. In the chaos of the coup the price of bread rose, and they starved. The people who had the flour made their fortunes. In early 1795, freezing weather froze the rivers and wolves came down from the hills to attack the poorest villagers and their animals. There was no relief when spring arrived because the thaw made the rivers flood their homes and fields. The peasant bellies were free: empty but free.

SYMPATHY – PHILIP CUNNINGHAM, 1804

You may not have a reason to revolt. But you see your fellow humans suffering and you offer them your support. Their cause isn't your cause but it's a good excuse to rise up against your own oppressors.

In 1804 Australia was the dumping ground for British criminals. Many of them coagulated into groups like blood brothers and sisters because they had the same origins. The Irish were one such group. Many of them were veterans of The United Irish rebellion of 1798 against their British oppressors. They only succeeded in becoming more oppressed.

Wolfe Tone had led his United Irishmen in a rising which was crushed. Apart from getting thirty thousand people killed, it also got Ireland's parliament abolished. Ireland would have direct rule imposed from London. 'Let that be a lesson to you,' was the message. But the Irish were never receptive to messages like that.

Some of their tactics in 1798 were original. The rebels wanted to attack Dublin under the cover of darkness, so they persuaded the lamplighters to go on strike. British soldiers thwarted this plan by using bayonets to persuade the lamplighters to go to work. Light relief.

In Wexford the rebels, led by priest Father John Murphy, had an early success. They crushed Irish loyalist defenders from Cork. The men from Cork pleaded for their lives. They pleaded in Irish – the principal language of the Gaeltacht region they came from – and the Wexford rebels didn't understand so they (understandably) shot them.

One of the most notorious incidents of the revolt was at Vinegar Hill near Wexford where the rebels captured thirty-five defenders and imprisoned them in a windmill. The captured men made a tactical mistake and complained of overcrowding. The rebel officer solved the problem by removing a dozen prisoners and having his men hack them to death with pikes.

When the rebels were defeated their punishment reflected their brutality. Father John Murphy was sentenced to be partially hanged (till he choked painfully), cut down alive, then to have his head cut off and stuck on a pole while his body was burnt in a tar barrel. (Father John had not learnt from Robespierre's demise about the wisdom of being merciful when you're winning.)

The allies of the United Irishmen, the French, finally invaded – too late and too little, with just a thousand men. Wolfe Tone was captured and sentenced to hang.

On the morning of his execution, he was found to have cut his windpipe with a penknife, but he had failed to cut the artery that would have let him bleed to death. The execution was put off. After a week of suffering a surgeon told Tone that if he tried to speak it would kill him. Tone replied, 'I can still find a word to thank you, sir. It is the most welcome news you could give me.' And he died.

But the rebellion wasn't over. A group of United Irishmen had fled to Paris. They returned in 1803, led by Robert Emmet. His rebellion was a sad failure when eighty men turned up to take Dublin Castle with just one ladder. Emmet was hanged, but he did not go down with glory. He climbed the hangman's ladder and had a rope placed around his neck but told the hangman not to take the ladder away till he dropped his handkerchief. His short speech went on too long and he failed to drop it, so the bored hangman grew tired of waiting and pushed Emmet off. After that, his head was cut off, but he was not disembowelled and quartered as the treason conviction required. He became another Irish martyr and an inspiration to followers as far away as Australia.

In 1804, some of the Irish rebels of the 1798 Tone and 1803 Emmet insurrections had been convicted and transported to Australia. Rather than accept defeat, they continued to fight for their cause in the Castle Hill rebellion. The Australian contingent was led by 1798 veteran Philip Cunningham. When the convict rebellion broke out he would be hailed as 'King of the Australian Empire.'*

Despite the brutality of the Australian penal colony there had been no uprisings against the authorities up to that point. There had been no unifying 'cause' strong enough to fight for. The United Irishmen's failed rebellions gave them one. The Irish convicts of 1804 had an audacious plan. They would overpower the government forces, set up an Irish colony in Australia then offer the freed convicts the option of staying on settler farms, or stealing ships, returning to Ireland and reigniting the rebellion that Tone and Emmet had died for.

The plan was to rally 1,800 convicts from camps in the region. On the evening of 4 March a leader of the rebel convicts, John Cavenah, set fire to his cabin as a signal to start the fight: a beacon that would light the way to freedom. Except it didn't. Few of the surrounding convict enclosures saw it so it turned out to be a damp squib. One group got lost as they tried to march through the dark and other convict couriers failed to get through with their messages. Planning was not a Castle Hill rebel forte.

In the end, only 233 convicts joined the rising. Even

---

* Technically we could argue that empires are overseen by an 'emperor' rather than a 'king' but Cunningham didn't live long enough to mount an imperial throne.

then they outnumbered the fifty-seven troops and settlers sent to arrest them. As well as stealing weapons, the rebels liberated large quantities of rum, which may have improved morale but been detrimental to their aim, don't you think?

The troops had the firepower. They also had the ruthlessness required. The rebel leader Philip Cunningham agreed to negotiations under a flag of truce. By now we know how that goes. The government officers pulled out their pistols and arrested him. This is just not cricket – not even Australian cricket. The rules of fair play were burnt to ashes. (A bit like John Cavenah's hut.) The troops then fired on the rebels, who fled. Under martial law the military were empowered to hang Cunningham very swiftly. Eight other convicts would join him on the gallows later. Two were hanged in chains or gibbeted, while seven were whipped with two hundred or five hundred lashes and sent to work on a chain gang.

About 150 rebels said they had never really wanted to be part of the rising but were bullied into it. True or not, it was a smart move and spared them more severe punishment. It was their get-out-of-jail-free card in some ways (obviously not in others).

Unsuccessful perhaps, but the Castle Hill rebellion went down in history as an action in sympathy with events twelve thousand miles away. Surely a record?

OPIUM WARS IN CHINA – LIN ZEXU, 1839

The British Empire never missed a chance to make a quick buck, no matter how immoral it was. In the 1830s the British traders from the East India Company had a good supply of opium, and they decided to stimulate business by creating a nation of addicts in China.

For a long time afterwards, Western countries would warn of those dangerous Chinese with their opium dens, from Oscar Wilde's *The Picture of Dorian Gray* to the hidden opium smuggling ring in the 1935 film *Charlie Chan in Shanghai*. In Arthur Conan Doyle's story 'The Man with the Twisted Lip', Dr Watson insinuates himself into an opium den to find a lost husband. And there he finds a disguised Sherlock Holmes. But don't worry, our national treasure was only gathering evidence for a case. Holmes himself would never indulge in the Chinese menace of opium, of course. (He preferred a 7 per cent solution of cocaine to stimulate his mind in boring lulls between cases. Don't try this at home.)

The Chinese nation was tarred with a brush wielded by the British traders, yet the locals were not passive in the face of the opium tsunami that swept across their nation in the 1800s.

At that time, China was seen as a partner for a British trade in sophisticated goods, a sort of nation of Bond Street suppliers, providing tea, silk, and porcelain.

Unfortunately, the Chinese showed little interest in British goods manufactured in the burgeoning Industrial Revolution. Britain was bleeding silver to pay for the luxury imports, so the merchants came up with a new 'currency' – opium, grown in British India. The local merchants accepted it in payment and sold it on at a profit. Demand was strong, since it is highly addictive. The initial pleasure soon becomes the avoidance of pain.

The Chinese government moved quickly to outlaw the drug, but it was too late. Corruption on the part of the Chinese enforcers and smuggling by the opium traders let the trade go on unabated.

Then, in 1839, the Daoguang Emperor chose a determined official called Lin Zexu to lead the rebellion against the British. Lin took radical measures in Canton (Guangzhou). He began by seizing and destroying over 2 million pounds of opium and then demanded that the merchants sign bonds promising to abandon the trade. He even blockaded the Portuguese colony of Macau, where British merchants were based.

But the British were as addicted to all that lovely money as the Chinese were to opium. First they had the effrontery to demand compensation for the destroyed drugs, even though they were illegal. The Chinese fought back, leading to the First Opium War (1839–42). As with so many rebellions, tech superiority prevailed and the British easily defeated the Chinese forces.

In a humiliating climbdown, the Chinese were forced to pay reparations and even to hand over Hong Kong

to the British. Worst of all, the peace terms legalized
the opium trade in China and created even more social
problems. Who could the Chinese blame for this
embarrassing failure? Lin Zexu, who else? He was sacked
and exiled.

We should give Lin Zexu credit. Before war had broken
out, he had written a famous letter to Empress Queen
Victoria herself. It quite logically pointed out . . .

> We have heard that in your own country opium is
> prohibited with the utmost strictness and severity.
> This is a strong proof that you know full well how
> hurtful it is to mankind. Since you do not permit it
> to injure your own country, you ought not to have the
> injurious drug transferred to our country.

Lin Zexu went on to say China's exports were all
harmless. 'Has China ever yet sent forth a noxious article
from its soil? Not to speak of our tea and rhubarb, things
which your foreign countries could not exist a single
day without.' The image of Queen Victoria struggling
to survive a day without rhubarb is one to savour. There
is no record of her responding. Not even to express her
amusement or lack thereof.

Lin Zexu would become a hero of China rather like
Hereward the Wake or Spartacus – someone who took on
a great oppressor and failed against insuperable odds. That
made it a glorious failure. He gave everything to the effort.
What more could anyone ask to have on their gravestone?

As with so many rebellions, the rebels emerged worse off than when they set out, and it was about to get still worse. The Second Opium War started with one of those silly 'how-very-dare-you' foot-stamps that became inflated to an absurd conflict. It became known as 'The Arrow Incident', and it was an excuse to squeeze still more concessions for the opium trade.

In 1856 a Chinese naval crew boarded a ship called *The Arrow*. The ship was Chinese owned but flew a British flag and was registered in Hong Kong. Cue outrage from the British. 'An insult to our flag, dontcha know. Damned foreign chappies need to be given a jolly good thrashing.' The British High Commissioner became impatient at the slowness of negotiations to settle the dispute, so he sent forces to the winter palace to loot and burn it down.

This time, the Brits had French and American allies. The French had lost several missionaries to Chinese executions – Christian preaching in several districts was forbidden by law (which the missionaries had ignored). The French had done nothing to defend their evangelists. But now they wanted an excuse for war, so they used the execution of their missionary Auguste Chapdelaine (1814–56) to seek reprisals too.

Mind you, it was a particularly brutal execution. The man was sentenced to 'cage torture': he was beaten one hundred times on the cheek by a leather thong. Not a simple slap on the face but a force that made his teeth sail out. He was locked in a small cage, suspended from the gate of the jail, and support was removed from his feet till he died from suffocation. His head was cut off and hung from a tree by his hair. Children with stones used it for target practice till Chapdelaine's head fell to the roadside and was fought over by stray dogs and pigs. That brought the French into the Second Opium War.

China was already struggling with the internal Taiping Rebellion, which cost the country between 20 and 30 million lives – as much as 10 per cent of the population, making it one of history's bloodiest revolutions. It was the Christian religion that had started it – a Chinese fanatic, Hong Xiuquan, declared he was the brother of Jesus Christ – so it is understandable why missionaries like Auguste Chapdelaine were outlawed.

Hong Xiuquan ended up so starved in a siege he died from eating weeds . . . or maybe he was poisoned. He joined his brother in heaven. The two could compare the relative merits of poisoning and crucifixion: twenty days for Hong to die, a few hours for Jesus. Hong's body was exhumed when the besieged city fell, dismembered and burnt. The ashes were blown from a cannon, which must have made an interesting encounter for St Peter at the gates of heaven.

The Opium Wars left China with a lasting resentment against Europe. Europe in turn demonized the Chinese. Scars like those take time to heal.

REASON TO REVOLT 9

WORK

'Deprived of meaningful work, men and women lose their reason for existence; they go stark, raving mad.'
FYODOR DOSTOEVSKY (1821–81) – RUSSIAN NOVELIST

The workplace is the home of a plethora of grievances that can erupt into revolt. Workers can come together into a union and be empowered to demand change. The workforce becomes a work force – forcing employers to change their ways. Pickets and strikes have often led to more work – more work for the undertakers. (Other unfortunates – like humble writers – work lonely and alone for a pittance and just have to suffer in their garrets and starve.)

And even worse than the evils of employment are the miseries of unemployment. No work = no income = no food = a slow death by starvation. In Georgian times a rural recession threw hundreds out of work. One emaciated family was found dead in a barn. When the corpses were dissected the stomachs were found to be filled with grass. Sometimes a revolution is needed.

BOSTON TEA PARTY - SAMUEL ADAMS, 1773

We pay taxes. Those taxes are used to benefit us in some way. One day they may even be used to fill that pothole outside your house. They also benefit the community in which we play no part. 'I have no children of school age,' you sigh, 'but I pay for the schooling system. I can't read (because that schooling system failed me) but my taxes are still used to pay for libraries. I pay for a police force so they can persecute me for exceeding the speed limit by one mile per hour, just because I drive a Lamborghini.' You know the sort of thing.

Taxes make sense, yet no one enjoys paying them. If we object to a particularly unfair tax – like VAT on books – then we can use our democratic right to vote out the fiend who created it. We have 'representation'. But if we had no say in an unfair tax then we may rebel and march under the banner of, 'No taxation without representation'. That is a particularly ugly slogan that doesn't scan and uses a lot of paint and cardboard. But in 1773 it is what the British settlers in America cried when they had a hissy fit about taxes.

They rose up against their British rulers in Britain which is, of course 'treason'. As the clever lines by Sir John Harington (1561–1612) said:

Treason doth never prosper. What's the reason?
Why, when it prospers, none dare call it treason.*

---

* Incidentally John Harington translated a rather rude poem into English then circulated it among his godmother, Elizabeth I's,

In other words, the Brits in America beat the Brits in Britain, so it isn't remembered in America as 'treason' or even a rebellion, but as a 'Revolution'.

The Brits in America were enraged by the 1773 Tea Tax. The Brits in Britain produced tea and were allowed to sell it directly to the Brits in America where it was taxed. The Brits in Britain needed that tax income to pay off war debts. The tea merchants in America were cut out of the loop and set to lose a packet. (The biggest losers were the American smugglers of Dutch tea who were going to be undercut by supplies of legitimate British tea.) A protest was called for.

The stereotypical American doesn't do irony, it has been said. But surely one or two of them must have raised an eyebrow when this land of slavers called their protest movement, 'The Sons of Liberty'. Or maybe that was just shorthand for 'The Sons of Liberty Not Counting Women, Native Americans or Imported Slaves'?

The revolt was led by men like American hero Samuel Adams . . . who some say was only acting in his self-interest. Sam is too dead to defend himself so let's judge him by his actions.

He was, when it all started, a failed businessman who had frittered away his inheritance from his rich father. Sam turned his attention to a fight for independence on the 'No taxation without representation' battle-cry, but it didn't start with tea, it started with sugar. The Sugar Act of 1764 had hit the colonists in their wallets. A year later the Stamp Act taxed most printed materials and

---

ladies-in-waiting, which caused quite a scandal. He also invented the flushing toilet. Lizzie was so impressed by the invention that when he gifted it to her, she forgave him. But I digress.

dialled up the temperature of colonial anger. The British enforcer of that tax was Andrew Oliver. The Americans hanged him (but it was in effigy, so it didn't hurt). His office was destroyed, as was the home of the governor.

The British authorities blamed Adams for stirring up the troubles and Adams defended himself by calling the destruction 'mobbish' which is an original and eloquent word. But the Stamp Act was repealed. The mobbish mob had made its mark where petitions and polite protests had failed.

It was time for the British to stop the rebels' destruction of its property and escalate their squeeze on the wallets. They sent in troops to Boston in 1768. They were intended as a 'peacekeeping' force, though they were about as good at keeping the peace as British soldiers in Northern Ireland during The Troubles. With the advantage of hindsight, we can see the way the British government was marching blindfolded into disaster.

In 1770 some of the peacekeeping soldiers in Boston took part-time jobs in the docks to supplement their income and that angered the locals. One soldier even wandered into a pub to ask if anyone knew of any jobs going. 'Unwise' would be an understatement. He was driven out and a mob gathered bent on revenge (one attacker later admitted they planned to murder him). When the soldier called for help the conflict escalated, as the arriving British soldiers were snowballed by the mob. Stones may have somehow been encased in the snow. The soldiers fired on the mob and five Americans were killed.

Independent witnesses say the protestors were asking for it. No, they literally asked for it, shouting into the faces of the armed party: 'Go on, fire. Damn you, you sons of bitches, fire.

Why don't you fire?' Other witnesses have said that a Bostonian called out, 'Fire'. So, they fired.

It became known as 'The Boston Massacre'. The first person to die was an escaped slave with the unusual name of Crispus Attucks, who is remembered as a martyr. The wound in his chest was described by a newspaper as 'goring the right side of his lungs, and a great part of the liver most horribly'. Samuel Adams campaigned to have the soldiers tried for murder. A couple of soldiers were found guilty of 'manslaughter' and branded on the thumb (which is not so painful as having your lungs gored). A quiet period followed but after the massacre many more Americans wanted real revenge, or better still, independence.

Yet it would take imagination to turn a single act of protest into an iconic moment in history. The Boston Tea Party. The American settlers wanted the tea ships sent back. The British governor in Boston refused to bow to the pressure and insisted the ships stay in harbour. The Bostonians held a meeting and decided they would retaliate to this provocation by dumping the shipload of tea into Boston Harbour. Poetic justice.

Some say that when Adams stated, 'This meeting can do nothing further to save the country', it was a coded message for the Tea Party to begin. Other say this story is a myth. Adams and his protest partners had come up with a rebel technique that has been imitated many times since. If you are going to protest, then do it in fancy dress. That not only makes it more memorable but also offers you a disguise in case your demo fails, and you are arrested. The disguise of choice was to dress as Mohawk warriors to carry out the attack. Today that would be considered something far worse than treason: 'cultural appropriation'.

In three hours, the Mohawk impersonators dumped all 342 chests of tea into the water and the legend was born.

The action was seized upon by Adams as a symbol of the liberty they were demanding. Not rebellion but defence of the settlers' rights – the Sons of Liberty were not the aggressors but the aggrieved. The British government overreacted again and demanded reparations. Adams helped arm the settlers to 'defend' their rights. The British ordered the arrest of Adams, and his Patriots believed he'd be hanged for treason. As the British army marched to follow their orders Adams escaped, the first shots were fired and the American Revolutionary War began.

The role of Adams in provoking the war is debatable. Some have said he not only planned the infamous Tea Party but also provoked the British into the Boston Massacre. How does that work? Did he approach a British occupying soldier (the enemy) and say, 'Hey, lad, pop into that pub and ask if there are any jobs going.'

The truth is Adams doesn't seem to have been the brightest squirrel in the nut factory. As well as failing in business he also failed miserably in one of his first jobs. If Americans did irony they would appreciate that, in this war against taxation, Samuel Adams was a failed what? Yes, tax collector. He frequently failed to collect from his fellow-citizens. (That made him very popular.)

He died in 1803, eulogized by some as 'The Father of the American Revolution' and others as the man who divided Britain from its friends in America. Sam's second cousin, John Adams, became the second president of the United States in 1797. Two centuries later, in 1985, Samuel Adams had a lager named after him.

THE *HERMIONE* MUTINY – CAPTAIN PIGOT, 1797

Sometimes 'progress' can work to the disadvantage of the workers. For spinners and weavers, industrial progress meant a wage reduction and unemployment. For sailors in the 1790s British navy, technological progress meant beating the barnacles.

Those little suckers had been plaguing ships since log canoes first sailed the oceans blue. (All right, slight exaggeration.) The mutiny on the *Bounty* may be the best remembered naval protest of the era, but the *Hermione* mutiny had the most lasting impact. For lovers of all things gory, it was also a lot bloodier. It even changed the course of American presidential history.

In the middle of a war against France and Spain, 150 members of the crew of HMS *Hermione* mutinied. The revolting crew comprised Irish and American seamen who were already anti-British to begin with before being press-ganged onto the ship. Conditions on board were cramped, the sailors were plagued by heat and pestilence, and they also weren't allowed off.

And that was where the barnacles came in. The creatures gathered on the wooden bottoms of ships and dragged at them like an anchor. Ships would have to land regularly to have them scraped off. These regular breaks were welcomed by the crews. Then along came some clever marine engineer who took HMS *Alarm*, a British frigate, and sheathed the hull with copper in 1758. It protected the hull against barnacles as well as shipworms. By the 1780s the idea was widely adopted and that was the end of regular shore leave for shellfish-smashing sailors. More time at sea, but no more pennies in the pay-packets.

Many ships suffered the same uncomfortable conditions as *Hermione* without mass murder and mutineers hanging from the yardarm. If you had to guess what went wrong on this ship you may look at the old *Mutiny on the Bounty* movie and think a sadistic captain like Captain Bligh had a hand (and a whip) in the rebellion. You would be right. Seven months before the *Hermione* mutiny, a new captain took command, twenty-eight-year-old Hugh Pigot, a young man unsuited to command. So how did he get the job? Family connections.

Pigot's infamy was earned by his predilection for frequent floggings.* Pigot didn't even have the courtesy to be predictable; his crew never knew when his cauldron of rage would boil over. In one incident, a popular young officer allowed a rope to be left untied on his watch. Not only was he demoted – a move that would wreck his naval career – but Pigot insisted he apologize on his knees and beg for forgiveness. The crew were angered by the needless humiliation.

Oh but Pigot had a wicked sense of humour. The day before the mutiny, a storm loomed on the horizon and Pigot gave the order for the sails to be furled (or rolled up if you are not marine-minded). That made sense and the sailors climbed the rigging to obey. But the corollary to the order was simply evil spite. He commanded, 'I shall flog the last man down.' Three of the sailors who had gone aloft fell fifty feet to their deaths in their panic to avoid punishment.

In sailor-speak, an inexperienced crew member would be

---

* No terrible puns, please, about flogged sailors moaning, 'The captain's got it in-fa-my.'

derided as a 'lubber'. Despite the fact that the three dead *Hermione* crew were experienced and respected sailors, Pigot coldly ordered that the 'lubbers' be thrown overboard. Other topmen received a flogging anyway.

As last straws go, that would break the toughest camel's back, yet Pigot piled on a hayrick the next morning. He ordered that a dozen men be flogged for 'lethargy'. That did it. Fuelled by stolen rum, they armed themselves with cutlasses and knives. After overpowering the guard on Pigot's cabin door they stabbed the captain and left him for dead ... which he wasn't. When they returned and found Pigot alive they plunged bayonets into him and threw him from the cabin window. His pitiful cries for help faded in the wake of the ship.

Eight more officers were murdered and thrown overboard, including Midshipman Smith, who was just fourteen years old. Their crime was to be tainted by association with Pigot. Lieutenant McIntosh had been dying of yellow fever when he was dragged from his bunk. It may have been Lieutenant Foreshaw who received the cruellest treatment. After he'd been forced overboard, he clung to the ship's rigging. He climbed back to the main deck and pleaded, 'Good God, what harm have I ever done to any of you?' Good question, to which the conscience-stricken crew had no answer. They promised mercy. But leading mutineer Thomas Nash raged, 'Foreshaw, you bugger. Are you not overboard yet? Overboard you must go, and overboard you shall go.' Foreshaw was thrown off the boat again.

The killers sailed into Spanish waters and handed the ship over to their Spanish enemies. Where were the officers? they were asked. 'Cast adrift in a small boat,' the crew lied. An echo of the mutiny on the *Bounty* around eight years earlier, when no one had died.

The incensed British navy conducted a manhunt and captured thirty-three mutineers, of whom twenty-four were hanged and gibbeted. But the fate of one would change the course of US history. The sadistic Thomas Nash claimed to be an American citizen called Jonathan Robbins, and said he'd been pressed by Hugh Pigot into the crew of *Hermione*. In 1799, President John Adams had him extradited to British Jamaica, where he was hanged. Cue outraged American voters. It cost Adams the 1800 election and the new president, Thomas Jefferson, swore no one would ever be extradited from the US, whether native American or asylum seeker. And for thirty-three years not one person was.

The *Hermione* mutiny changed the world, but not in the way Nash and his mutineers could ever have dreamt. It was the deadliest mutiny in British naval history but compared to other 1797 mutinies it is all but forgotten. Two more famous mutinies happened at Spithead and the Nore, though they were relatively polite 'strikes'. In April, at Spithead, an anchorage near Portsmouth, sailors refused to sail because of poor pay and conditions – and that copper-bottomed reduction of shore leave. The negotiations were successful, and pardons granted.

The following month the Nore strike at the mouth of the Thames could have had a similar outcome. The government offered pardons to the strikers, but some pushed their luck and held out, blockading the Thames. Their leader was Richard Parker, who came up with an original defence when he was sent for trial: 'I didn't know the mutineers had elected me as their leader.' Nice try, Richard. He was hanged along with twenty-eight other mutineers.

MACHINE WRECKING – NED LUDD, 1812

Technology changes our world, and the march of the machines seems unstoppable, from the inventors of fire and the wheel – neither of which were patented at the time – up to today's artificial intelligence. Those pitiful little animals (a.k.a. humans) invent the equivalent of a steamroller with no brakes, thinking they can jump on and steer it down the endless slope they call 'time'. But they delude themselves. Every time.

They invent the printing press to mass-produce books. They congratulate themselves that they have given their fellow creatures *Hamlet*. Then they realize they have also given us *Mein Kampf*. And they are so busy looking at the glorious future they fail to see what they are leaving in their wake – squashed under the steamroller, usually. Printing also became a way of disseminating rebellious ideas. The ruling classes were always wary that a literate underclass would be persuaded to rebel against them. Bibles were printed and put in the hands of the priests but they were printed in Latin so the church stayed in control. John Wycliffe's translations of the Bible were burnt by the Catholic Church. Just to make sure rebel readers got the message, Wycliffe's corpse was dug up and burnt too.

William Tyndale translated the Bible and in 1526, Henry VIII's Bishop Tunstall ordered copies to be publicly burnt in London. Over in Belgium they didn't bother to dig him up and burn his corpse – they put the gravedigger out of work and burnt

Tyndale at the stake in 1536. (He was strangled first so he didn't suffer, so that's all right.)

That printing press has put the monks out of the copying business and sentenced many others to the scrap-heap of the past: the parchment-makers, the quill-sharpeners and the ink-pot potters.

They had to be re-trained as publishers and editors, agents and sales reps, librarians and the gnomes who labour in the caverns they call bookshops. And then . . . then . . . they put many of those wage-slaves out of business by inventing electronic screens. Soon AI will write the books and even writers will be redundant. It's no use telling an author they can make a living as a bus-conductor when they've never done an honest day's work in their life. Eventually, even you, the reader, will be excluded. At least your noise-cancelling earphones will drown out the piteous cries of the impoverished and starving writers. Historians will add to the lamentations, 'Ned Ludd, we know how you felt.'

The rebel followers of legendary weaver Ned Ludd in the late 1700s and early 1800s were not the first (and will be far from the last) to see their lives destroyed by new technology, but they are among the best remembered. Their name is a byword for futile attempts to roll back the steamroller of progress: Luddite.

Earlier in the century, Daniel Defoe (1660–1731) had placed the British in seven categories, from super-rich to destitute. The spinners and weavers were bang in the middle: 'The Working Trades – who labour hard but feel no want'. That was about to change. The self-employed may have 'felt no want' but it wasn't much of a life. Spinners worked fourteen hours a day in steamy temperatures up to 90°F (32°C) – it had to be steamy to stop the thread snapping. The weavers were better paid and could earn two to three pounds a week when Defoe was writing. Builders built houses in the cloth-producing towns especially for weavers. They were built over ditches so the weavers could work in a nice damp cellar. It ruined their health, but at least the threads didn't snap.

The 'flying shuttle' was invented in 1733 by John Kay. Cloth could be woven faster and wider. Weavers could produce twice as much every day – the weak link was the spinners, who were unable to keep up the pace with the production of the yarn. There was some resistance to Kay's invention but nothing violent. Kay wisely went to France to sell his looms and avoid confrontation.

As with so many inventions, the development was shifted up several gears by another new technology that built on the last, like the difference between propellor aeroplanes and jet engines. In 1798, the new steam engines came along to power the looms that made cloth. The old problem of the yarn suppliers with their spinning wheels had been solved around 1764 by James Hargreaves, a weaver and carpenter from Lancashire. Spinning wheels produced one thread at a time, whereas Hargreaves's spinning jenny was a multi-spindle spinning machine. (Try saying 'multi-spindle spinning machines' after a pint of Lancashire ale.)

Now eight spindles could be spun simultaneously and (very important) by one operator. Supply could meet the demand of the thread-hungry steam-powered looms. The cloth manufactured by machines was produced faster and more cheaply than that of human workers. In 1775, Richard Arkwright's water frame made still finer, stronger yarn and was powered by waterwheel, requiring even fewer human skills.

The Luddite movement is remembered as a rebellion in the

Nottinghamshire clothing factories of 1811. In fact, Glaswegian protestors pre-dated the Notts workers by more than twenty years.

The price of cloth in Scotland fell in 1787 and clothes became cheaper. Joy for anyone who wore clothes, except the weavers who got less money for their work. Men, women and children worked six days for eighteen shillings. Weavers in the Calton district of Glasgow had to sell their bedclothes to buy food. Misery.

The Calton weavers who made muslin cloth had two pay cuts in 1787. At the same time the price of food was going up. Inflation hurts the poorest most, like these weaving families, who had no savings. There are just two words in the English language ending in -ngry. They are 'hungry' and 'angry'. The Calton weavers were both. Their response was quite restrained at first. They went on strike. This was one of the first strikes in British history.

A strike is no use if you stay in bed and sulk. If you've sold your bedclothes to pay for food it won't be very comfortable either. You have to get out there and draw attention to your plight. The Calton weavers gathered a large crowd, of about seven thousand workers, and marched on Glasgow Green to tell the council leaders they wanted better wages. Their pleas fell on deaf ears because the council leaders were the wealthy burghers of the city. As the writer G. K. Chesterton said . . .

Among the rich you will never find a really generous man even by accident . . . they are egoistic, secretive, dry as old bones. To be smart enough to get all that money you must be dull enough to want it.

The weavers got nothing, so the strike went on for weeks and everyone got hungrier and angrier. It was time for direct action, and the first thing most revolting people need is a target on which to vent their spleen. Some of the striking workers broke into the factories and cut the threads on the power looms operated by the few who had refused to strike. The principal targets were the warehouses where the cloth was stored. The cloth was taken out then burnt in the streets.

Troops were called in. They were probably local militia and as scared of the mob as they were of the Glasgow council leaders who sent them in. Scared soldiers panicked. If they ever planned to fire over the heads of the revolting weavers then they missed. Six weavers died and are considered the first working-class martyrs of the Industrial Revolution.

The strike failed but the battle against the machines went on ... and the weavers went on losing. One of the strike leaders, James Granger, was charged for the riots. He was whipped through the streets by the Glasgow executioner. He was then told not to return. After his exile he came back and took part in another strike in 1811.*

Machines did more and more of the work. They could be worked by women and even children who were unskilled but cheap. This phenomenon has been repeated ever since – machines becoming so 'user-friendly' almost anyone can operate them. That is not to say the looms of the 1800s were friendly, exactly. They were highly dangerous. Those cute little children were small

---

* You will not be astonished to learn that the murderous soldiers were not punished.

and nimble enough to clean and repair machinery while it was running. The gears and belts of these monsters would devour fingers, hands and even limbs. Getting hair tangled in the cogs would mean loss of hair and/or loss of life.

Weavers tried wrecking the machines that were taking their jobs. Male weavers attacked female weavers to get their jobs. Others stole scraps of cloth and thread to sell to feed their families. Child labour came from the Glasgow workhouse and the youngsters worked all day. The growth of these five- to eight-year-olds was stunted and they were often too tired to eat. One report said children were too tired to even dress themselves in the morning. A single factory had more than five hundred children working there. Glasgow was the worst place for child cruelty in Britain. One owner said, 'They come from poor families and need the money the children bring. I am doing good.' He could sleep well with a clear conscience then, and even manage to dress himself in the morning.

The first major Nottinghamshire attacks occurred in 1811 and targeted the wide knitting frames that produced lower-quality goods. This event is often quoted as the start of the Luddite rebellions. But you know otherwise. They were just rebellions that were tagged with the name of the leader, Ned Ludd.

Ned Ludd was said to be a young apprentice who first began destroying textile apparatus in 1779. The subsequent machine-wreckers said they were taking orders from 'General Ludd'. The truth is there is no evidence that Ludd existed. He is as historical as Robin Hood.

The 1811 confrontations spread the next year, with a typical example being the attack on William Cartwright's mill at

Rawfolds near Huddersfield. It was met by an armed body of men. They killed two attackers and were praised by the local press. A Leeds newspaper wrote that 'it's unnecessary to speak of the heroism of the little band that guarded these premises, there is not perhaps upon record a more distinguished instance of manly courage and cool intrepidity'. The reporter probably got a free year's supply of cloth for that. The dead, on the other hand, were held up as an example to would-be machine-wreckers; putative Luddites were warned, 'Let them recollect that they themselves may be the next victims and let them stop in this desperate career before it is too late.'

If newspapers can shape public opinion then the reports on Luddite attacks were never going to elicit sympathy for the wreckers. The Luddite riots of 1811 had been extinguished by 1813. Hangings and transportations – along with the weariness and weakness of hunger – sapped the will of the rebels. Yet in the darkness there were flickers of humanity. Thomas Duckworth, a sixteen-year-old handloom weaver from Lancashire, reported that his party of strikers met soldiers with drawn swords. Duckworth said: 'Some of the old fellows from the mob spoke. They said "What are we to do? We're starving. Are we to starve to death?" The soldiers were fully equipped with haversacks, and they emptied their sandwiches among the crowd.'

As Scottish rhymester Rabbie Burns had put it in 1784,

Man's inhumanity to man
Makes countless thousands mourn.

But just occasionally, man's humanity to man shines through.

HOIST THE FLAG

'There is no crueller tyranny than that which is perpetuated under the shield of law and in the name of justice.'

MONTESQUIEU (1689–1755) – FRENCH PHILOSOPHER

The French Revolution rebels wore the Phrygian cap and the Wang Mang opponents adopted Red Eyebrows. If you want to lead a revolution then you may want to adopt some sign that will identify you and symbolize your cause.

FLAGS

The Jolly Roger: Also known as the 'Captain Death' flag, the Jolly Roger was a sign of pirates who defied the laws. Late seventeenth-century pirate John Avery (a.k.a Long Ben or Henry Every and active between 1694 and 1696) was one of the first to use this as his symbol. Contrary to all TV shows, they were often red; the name is derived from the French *'jolie rouge'* or 'fine red' flag. These flags were often decorated with bones and skulls and were used the way a red traffic light is used, to say 'Stop or suffer the consequences'.

The Gadsden Flag: This yellow flag had the image of a rattlesnake and the sensible advice 'Don't tread on me'. It was created by Christopher Gadsden (1724–1805), an American general during the Revolution. Before the war, Britain proposed sending convicted criminals to their American colonies. Benjamin Franklin said the Americans should reciprocate this generous act by sending rattlesnakes to Britain. The rattlesnake became a symbol of the revolution and hence the flag. The snake's thirteen rattles represented the thirteen colonies.

King George III's troops must have cringed when they saw the yellow flag fluttering from Gadsden's flagship, for the message 'Dont tread on me' omitted the apostrophe. An early example of Americans murdering the English language.

The Red Flag: Red has become a symbol of revolution. Like the USA's 'star-spangled banner', the Red Flag has had a song dedicated to it, sung to this day at meetings of the British Labour party by those who can remember the words. The gruesome lyrics suggest red is the blood of the movement's martyrs. But don't be too depressed because it is sung to the tune of 'Lauriger Horatius', better known as the German carol, 'O Christmas Tree'. The 1889 lyrics of Irishman Jim Connell were not especially Christmassy:

The people's flag is deepest red,
It shrouded oft our martyred dead,
And ere their limbs grew stiff and cold,
Their hearts' blood dyed its every fold.
Then raise the scarlet standard high.
Within its shade we'll live and die,
Though cowards flinch and traitors sneer,
We'll keep the red flag flying here.

You could try singing 'Old Santa's coat is deepest red' but you may be ejected from the party. Stick to Mr Connell's version.

The Black Flag: Black can represent both rebellion and mourning. The mourning is for liberty lost. Many anarchist groups since the 1880s have adopted it. But the first black flags of revolt were probably raised in France in 1831. The silk weavers saw their wages fall and marched on Lyon under the black flag in the Canut revolt.

When the Paris Commune tried to rise up against the government in 1871, Louise Michel – a leader of the Paris Commune – wrote, 'The black flag is the flag of strikes and the flag of those who are hungry.' Under the black flag she led a protest march crying, 'Bread, work or lead.' (The lead of bullets for their opponents.)

The Paris Commune was an attempt at self-government by the people of Paris. The government sent in troops who killed or executed up to fifteen thousand men and women fighting under the black flag. Of course, the establishment supporters suffered too. The commune executed the Archbishop of Paris in an echo of the English Peasants' Revolt almost five hundred years before when Simon Sudbury, Archbishop of Canterbury, was beheaded. Shakespeare wrote, 'Uneasy lies the head that wears a crown.' He could have added, 'or the mitre.'

SYMBOLS

The Black Cat: The origin of the Black Cat is a sweet story. In 1905 the Industrial Workers of the World in America held a strike that was going badly. Members suffered beatings that put several in hospital. Into the strikers' camp wandered a malnourished black cat. The strikers fed it and saw the cat regain its strength. From that time onward, the strikers scored some notable victories, including wage rises. That would pay for the investment in cat food then. They adopted the cat as the symbol of their movement.

The Black Hand: The Black Hand Gang sounds like a cartoon invention for a children's comic or an opponent of Richard Hannay in the John Buchan thrillers from the first half of the twentieth century. But it really existed, and its members caused untold misery for the world. The aim of the gang was to unite the territories where Serbians lived and free them from occupation by the Austro-Hungarian Empire. In 1914 the Austrians (rather unwisely) sent Archduke Franz Ferdinand, the heir to

237

the throne, to Bosnia on a state visit. Six of the seven incompetent Black Hand assassins failed to kill him. The seventh – Gavrilo Princip – succeeded. It was the match to the fuse that ignited the First World War.

The Black Hand Gang didn't just sound like an invention of Dennis the Menace – even their secret oath was melodramatic:

> I do hereby swear by the Sun which shineth upon me, by the Earth which feedeth me, by God, by the blood of my forefathers, by my honour and by my life, that from this moment onward and until my death, I shall faithfully serve the task of this organisation.

> But the result of their action was far from funny – unless you enjoy black comedy.

REASON TO REVOLT 10

INJUSTICE

'There is no grievance that is a fit object
of redress by mob law.'

ABRAHAM LINCOLN (1809–65) – AMERICAN PRESIDENT

We all have grievances when we feel we've been treated unjustly – whether it is your neighbour's cat digging up your beloved geraniums or that myopic referee that cost your football team the match. These storms of life are confined to your teacup and should not result in a loss of life – yours or next-door's cat's.

But other injustices are on a scale that hundreds or thousands share. They have a common cause, and they come together with a quest for justice in mind. When mob law takes over then the enemies are those in authority – or the symbols of their oppression. Those symbols can take the shape of a postbox or a parliament. The mob isn't fussy.

THE SWEDISH AMBASSADOR – LOUIS XIV, 1661

Historically, small grievances have led to violence and death – for horses and plasterers.

On 30 September 1661 the new Swedish ambassador was arriving in London and King Charles II's barge would collect him from Gravesend. He'd be rowed up the Thames to the wharf at the Tower of London and transfer to the Swedish carriage. His carriage would then follow the King's carriage to a reception at Whitehall. Crowds gathered in their thousands. Did they want to see the spectacle? No. They wanted to witness a fight.

The dispute would be over who followed the Swedish carriage. There were two contenders for third in line: the Spanish and the French. To them, it was a matter of precedence. The greater country would take its place behind the Swedish carriage. Charles II knew there would be a fierce rivalry on occasions like this, so he might have solved it by inviting neither France nor Spain. But the rival ambassadors were such senior aristocrats Charles had no choice.

King Louis XIV of France had ambitions to be the ruler of a united Europe (even though united Europe is an oxymoron). Conquering the Spanish Netherlands would be high on Louis's hit list. But first he needed to win the battle of precedence in the London parade. His representatives were clearly instructed to give no ground. On the Spanish side they clearly anticipated Ibárruri's imprecation: 'They shall not pass.'

Charles knew there would be trouble but the best he could do was issue an edict: any English person getting involved would be punished by death. There was no edict against most of London gathering to witness the international showdown. Naturally the spectators would have favourites. The diarist Samuel Pepys noted, 'We do naturally all love the Spanish, and hate the French.' Given that the Anglo-Spanish war of 1585 to 1604 was in living memory, that is a dubious claim. But ultimately, the spectators didn't care who won because one of the old enemies would lose. It would be more fun than a public hanging.

The rival aristocrats promised Charles II there would be no firearms involved. Bladed weapons were not excluded.

The Swedish ambassador was due to arrive at three o'clock. An eyewitness set the scene . . .

Tower-Hill was not just filled with spectators, but also plenty of armed guards on foot and horseback in order to prevent the spectators from getting involved in the possible carnage.

Both sides tried to jump the gun. The French carriage arrived four hours early, only to find the Spanish had arrived five hours early and was guarded by fifty men with swords. The French had brought a hundred infantry and another fifty on horseback. The French also cheated because their musketeers had brought pistols and carbines. Where was a referee when you needed one?

As 3 p.m. approached, the crowd's expectations reached fever pitch. Their lust for blood would be sated. The Swedish ambassador's carriage took its place. The national anthems of the two sides were not played. The Spanish angled themselves on the wharf to block the French. One of history's first explosions of road rage was about to occur. The thwarted French attacked with sword and pistol. The outnumbered Spanish held them off but at a cost to both sides: three horses, a postilion and the French coachman were killed. The horses were collateral damage, but the French could always eat them later.

The Spanish used the mayhem to jockey their carriage behind the Swedish and the procession was off and running. Spain one, France nil. But the French still had subs to bring on. Armed men were in position on Tower Hill and now joined the fray. They targeted the harness of the Spanish carriage, but the Spanish had anticipated that; they had used iron traces under the leather. Spain two, France nil.

The sorry French carriage trailed behind half an hour later with just two remaining horses. Estimates say twelve of the rivals died and forty were wounded. One extra victim was an English plasterer who was hit in the head by a stray French bullet (from a pistol that the French had promised not to carry).

Louis XIV had lost the battle but won a huge justification to go to war with his rivals. 'Apologize or I shall annexe the Netherlands', he cried in mock rage. Spain not only apologized but agreed that France would always have precedence in diplomatic situations and if that if they ever broke that promise then Louis XIV could have the Netherlands.

The Spanish ambassador was sent to France to apologize in the glare of a spectacular reception while other European ambassadors and even the Pope's representative watched the humiliation. A medal was struck to commemorate the victory. Louis had come up with a late hat-trick and the game ended Spain two, France three.

Thirteen dead (not forgetting the horses) for what appeared to be a petty squabble over precedence was in fact an engineered diplomatic incident. The apparent winners were the Spanish, when in fact they emerged the losers.

How could that happen, the Spanish supporters would demand. There would be an inquisition.

THE AMERICAN CIVIL WAR – JOHN WILKES BOOTH, 1862

The plantation owners in the southern states of the US didn't need slaves (no one does) but not paying any wages certainly made the plantations more profitable. Fortunately, the southern states, the Confederates, lost on the battlefield in the American Civil War. Unfortunately, they focused their resentment on one man from the northern Union: Abraham Lincoln. He was a distinctive figure and a clear target for the Confederates, who were not going to take defeat with good grace.

Assassinate Lincoln and you are not going to reverse the defeat. You've lost: get over it and move on. That was not how the Confederates felt. They were nursing their grievance, and some avenger was going to target Lincoln. The man who got there first was John Wilkes Booth and he had another driving force: ego.

Booth came from a celebrated theatrical family. When he set out on the path of assassination he spoke theatrically: 'Liberty, liberty. How many crimes are committed in thy name?'

He also craved fame the way so many thespians do. He wanted to live and be remembered as a hero and a saviour. He was sent

by God, he claimed. 'I can never repent. God made me the instru-
ment of His punishment.' Delusions of grandeur made him a
dangerous person. But he was not suicidal. He wanted to live to
enjoy his notoriety.

When he was a schoolboy, a fortune-teller had tried to warn
him that he would have 'a grand but short life, doomed to die
young and meeting a bad end'. Oddly, his victim had an equally
accurate premonition.

The morning before he was assassinated, Lincoln awoke from
a nightmare and asked his wife, 'Mary, do you believe you can see
the future in dreams?'

She snorted. 'Nonsense, Mr Lincoln. What sort of dream have
you had?' He told her:

A dream of death, Mary. It was so real. It all started here.
I knew I was in bed asleep but then I dreamed that I woke
up. When I listened carefully I heard wailing and weeping
coming from downstairs. I got out of bed to see what
was happening. In my dream I went downstairs here and
looked in every room. They were all empty. At last, I came
to the East Room, and it was guarded by two soldiers. I
looked through the door and there were all my friends
gathered around the table sobbing. They were gathered
around a coffin. There was a body in the coffin, dressed in
funeral clothes. I couldn't make out his face because it was
covered with a cloth. So, I turned and asked a soldier who
had died. The soldier told me it was President Lincoln in
that coffin . . . and he'd been shot by an assassin. It was me,
Mary. Me.

Mary Lincoln tried to reassure him that Abe was a hero, and no one would want to kill him. He pointed out, 'I'm not a hero in the south.'

He had none of the suffocating protection that today's politicians have, and even now attackers still get through. President Kennedy was hit by a long-range sniper. British political activist Nigel Farage was struck in the face with an avenging banana milkshake in 2024. In the same year President Donald Trump on the campaign trail had his ear nicked by a bullet which sped on to kill one of his audience. No one is safe. When Lincoln went to the Ford's Theatre in Washington with minimal protection, he had no chance. A single police officer guarded the door to his box seat.

The people saw little of their president that night. He sat back in the box in a rocking chair and watched the play wearily. It was a comedy, *Our American Cousin*. The audience were enjoying it. Even Mary laughed. But Abraham Lincoln was tired to the marrow of his bones and the horror of the previous night's dream hung over him in the shadows.

And from those deep shadows stepped John Wilkes Booth. He couldn't believe his luck. He had crept up the stairs to the door. The president's guard had grown bored and slipped away for a drink. When Booth tried the door it was unlocked. He opened it silently and stood a pace behind the man he hated. The president and his guests looked down on the brightly lit stage. The actor on the stage called to another, 'You sockdologizing old man-trap.' The audience roared with laughter.

That was the moment Booth had waited for. He knew the play. He had timed it so he would arrive here at this very moment.

Now he raised the pistol, placed it behind the president's ear and pulled the trigger. The small gun wasn't as loud as the cheering audience. At first Mary Lincoln didn't realize what had happened. All she knew was that a man rushed past her and jumped up to the ledge that overlooked the stage.

'Freedom for the South!' he cried before he jumped down.

Booth could have escaped by running back through the unguarded door to the box as soon as he'd fired. But he was seeking glory. He wanted to be remembered for this moment; he was a luvvie desperate for attention. So, he made a stupid gesture. He jumped onto the stage. His dramatic line was well rehearsed: 'Sic semper tyrannis. The South is avenged.'* The audience were confused. Apart from the fact not many knew Latin, some wondered if this was part of the play. Many laughed, some gasped and others fell silent. As the strange man with the pistol limped off the stage they looked up to the balcony where a small, moon-faced woman looked down on them and screamed, 'The president. Mr Lincoln. He's been shot!'

President Lincoln died the following morning. And Booth's leap to the stage had broken his leg. Such a notorious man, on the run with a price on his head, would have small chance of escape. A man on the limp had no chance. Sure enough, Booth was caught ten days later as he headed for the southern states. He died in a gunfight with the soldiers sent to arrest him.

---

* The Latin phrase, meaning 'thus always to tyrants', was associated with the assassination of Julius Caesar. Booth, who had once stated that his favourite Shakespearean character was Brutus, was claiming his place in history.

John Wilkes Booth wanted to be remembered. So let us remember him as a nasty little bigot who killed for spite. He claimed, 'I have too great a soul to die like a criminal.' He was wrong. Let's remember the attention-seeking racist who urged Americans, 'It is our duty to see that this country is not overrun by a negro population.' And now that we've remembered him, let's forget him. He's not worth the brain space.

THE SUFFRAGETTES – EMILY DAVISON (1872–1913)

John Edward Acton wrote a letter to Bishop Mandell Creighton in 1887 in which he made the frequently misquoted statement, 'Power tends to corrupt, and absolute power corrupts absolutely. Great men are almost always bad men.' The 'tends to' is often omitted.*

Acton's second sentence is usually forgotten. But it's significant. Power makes you bad, which is a fair point. But the other totally ignored word is 'men'. Not 'women'. For the 50 per cent of the population that identify as female have always struggled to attain power over their own lives, let alone their contemporaries'. And the male half of the world has been so corrupted they have fought desperately to hold on to and enforce their 'absolute power'. For thousands, and tens of thousands of years, women have been disempowered or been obliged to wield their influence behind the scenes.

---

* Maybe we should give credit to Prime Minister William Pitt the Elder (in power 1766–68), who allegedly said in Parliament that 'unlimited power is apt to corrupt the minds of those who possess it'.

When the Chartists were battling for the vote in the 1830s it was the vote for men, never women. And when women began to voice their anger and demand the vote, their protests were crushed with excessive cruelty. Men held the power and power corrupted their sense of equality. If there were ever a 'good' excuse for revolting then it was the battle for women to be acknowledged as the equal of men.

The wily women knew they couldn't win their war with a trial of strength, and polite petitions would get them nowhere. They needed a campaign of civil disobedience that would draw attention to their cause and shame the men in power. They wanted the vote – suffrage – so they were suffragists. However, a reporter at the *Daily Mail* wanted to belittle the movement so he labelled them suffragettes, indicating 'little' suffragists.

Women over twenty-one on the Isle of Man had got the vote in 1881, but they had to be unmarried – once they married, the man of the house could make the decisions on the little woman's behalf. New Zealand women over twenty-one had got the vote in 1893. When British women still had no vote ten years later, Emmeline Pankhurst set up the Women's Social and Political Union (WSPU) in Manchester and began to recruit like-minded women.

Emmeline insisted that '"Deeds, not words" was to be our permanent motto.' Those 'deeds' included heckling political leaders like Winston Churchill and demanding to know where he stood on women's suffrage. They were charged with a technical assault on a policeman, refused to pay the fine and were sent to prison. Naturally the publicity this attracted was manna to the WSPU. Some of their tactics were innovative; in 1909 two suffragettes tried to engineer a meeting with Prime Minister Asquith by sending themselves by Royal Mail courier post to Downing Street. A first-class idea, but Downing Street declined the parcel. Maybe they hadn't put enough stamps on?

After nearly ten years the campaign was making little headway and parts of the WSPU wanted more violent action – an idea which split the alliance. They began . . .

+ smashing windows,
+ chaining themselves to railings
+ setting fire to letters in postboxes
+ burning politicians' unoccupied homes
+ burning the words VOTES FOR WOMEN into golf-course greens
+ flying an airship over London emblazoned with their motto and dropping leaflets

Some observers tried to argue that damaging property was counterproductive and alienated potential supporters. They still say that to this day when (for example) climate protestors bring a halt to motorway traffic and misery for thousands.

But there was an especially vicious quashing of a suffragette protest. At one march hundreds were badly hurt, and the police violence caused some deaths. This day became known as Black Friday. Alienating supporters? Emmeline Pankhurst wisely pointed out . . .

Public conscience must be aroused, and it can only be done by attacks on public property. When women's bodies were battered on Black Friday that was alright but when a few windowpanes are broken, that is all wrong.

Then it escalated to more extreme action: a bombing campaign. Government offices, churches and public buildings were targeted. Letter bombs and assassination attempts had to be taken seriously. At least four people died.

If the action escalated then so did the punishments. Attempts to go on hunger strike in prison were dealt with by forced feeding. A tube through the nostril or a stomach pump (in reverse) ensured the women didn't die and become a martyr for the cause. It was brutally painful, yet Evaline Burkitt was force-fed 292 times in five years. But the suffragettes would get their martyr another way.

It was Emily Davison who had devised the plan to set fire to postboxes. She began taking increasingly confrontational actions, which prompted Sylvia Pankhurst – the daughter of Emmeline – to describe Emily as 'one of the most daring and reckless of the militants'. She was about to prove it.

She graduated from breaking windows and setting fire to postboxes to hiding in the Houses of Parliament overnight (three times); she lasted longer in there than Guy Fawkes had. Not all of her actions were well-judged. She attacked a Baptist minister on a train with a horsewhip; she had mistaken him for the politician David Lloyd George. That was no way to whip up support. Her maverick actions were starting to embarrass the leadership of the WSPU.

She suffered being force-fed forty-nine times when arrested. She said, 'The experience will haunt me with its horror all my life and is almost indescribable. The torture was barbaric.' But 'all my life' would not be as long as anyone would have expected. In

1912 she attempted suicide in prison by throwing herself over a balcony onto an iron staircase, but she was caught by netting put there to prevent such an action. She later explained . . .

> I did it deliberately and with all my power, because I felt that by nothing but the sacrifice of human life would the nation be brought to realise the horrible torture our women face. If I had succeeded I am sure that forcible feeding could not in all conscience have been resorted to again.

And that statement makes her death problematic. To this day her act on 4 June 1913 divides opinion. Davison collected two flags in the suffragette colours of purple, white and green. She went to Epsom by train to attend the horse race of the year, the Derby. She took up a position at the final bend of the course, ducked under the rail and ran towards the horse Anmer, owned by King George V. She was clutching her flags and appears to reach for the horse's reins. The incident was captured by three cine-cameras, and you can still watch it today.

If she was trying to halt a ton of horseflesh travelling at 35mph then she failed. The horse smashed into her, and she fell, fracturing her skull. She never regained consciousness and died two days later. Among the get-well-soon messages there was hate-mail from analogue trolls. The King, who had attended the race, was unsympathetic and called it 'scandalous'. His dear queen was even more forthright and told her diary that Davison was a 'horrid woman'. No suffrage support from Queen Mary then.

The coroner's verdict was 'accident'. Supporters of that verdict will tell you that . . .

+ Davison had a return rail ticket in her pocket – she expected to go home.
+ The film shows she doesn't throw herself under the hooves but reaches for the bridle.
+ It appears she carried the flags with a view to attaching them.

Those who would prefer to see Emily Davison as a willing martyr for women's suffrage point out that . . .

+ A highly intelligent person like Emily could not expect to survive such an impossible stunt.
+ She was proven to be mentally unbalanced by the repeated 'barbaric torture'.
+ The suicide attempt in prison indicated martyrdom was her intent.

The First World War that put pause to the suffrage fight oddly helped them – women won respect for throwing themselves behind the military with their war work. In 1918, Parliament granted the vote to propertied women over the age of thirty. Ten years later, the voting age for women was lowered to twenty-one to put them on equal terms with male voters.

Today's women still struggle to be accepted on 'equal terms' with men; it remains a revolution waiting to happen. Power tends to corrupt, and men still hold the balance of power. But we live in hope. William Golding, the author of *Lord of the Flies*, said, 'I think women are foolish to pretend they are equal to men. They are far superior and always have been. Whatever you give a woman, she will make greater.'

Emily didn't live to see the suffragette cause triumph, but in 2021 the flag she carried was auctioned and now hangs in Parliament – the Parliament she had no right to enter.

LESSONS FROM HISTORY 10

LAST WORDS

'I cannot be a traitor, for I owe the English king no allegiance. He is not my Sovereign; he never received my homage; and whilst life is in this persecuted body, he never shall receive it.'

(LAST WORDS OF) WILLIAM WALLACE (C. 1270–1305) – SCOTTISH LEADER*

There are 'good' causes worth revolting for: the unselfish, the struggle against oppression in our world of wars, poverty and plagues. There are 'bad' causes where the rebels want to strengthen their power over the weak, enrich themselves or inflict misery for sport.

But when you decide to become revolting – more revolting than you already are – it is important that you think of your legacy. As you lie on your deathbed, crushed by the tanks of the tyrants you were fighting, someone like me will be sitting there with a notebook (or a recording device) to jot down your last words. Your last words may

---

* Not the *Braveheart* movie invention, 'They may take our lives, but they'll never take our freedom.'

just inspire future generations to succeed where you failed so miserably when that tank ran over your foot.

I'd suggest you prepare yourself for that moment and start creating your 'last words' now. Need some inspiration? Have a look at what your revolting predecessors or their victims said/gasped/croaked.

HUGH LATIMER – BURNT BY MARY TUDOR, 1555

If you are going to die slowly for your rebellion then plan something memorable. If you can manage a clever play on words then your admirers will be impressed by your literary skills as well as your example.

Hugh Latimer was sent to the stake by Mary Tudor for the sin of being a Protestant. He had been a passionate opponent of Protestantism in the 1520s when he heard the confessions of Protestant Thomas Bilney before *he* was burnt at the stake. Bilney converted Latimer to Protestantism. As cleric Thomas Fuller would say a century later, 'Nothing is more zealous than a convert.'

Several high-profile Protestants were executed for refusing to renounce their faith. Along with Hugh Latimer, another leading rebel was Nicholas Ridley. Latimer was tied to the stake back-to-back with Ridley . . . which saved on fuel. Fry one get one free. He spoke his famous last words to Ridley: 'Play the man, Master Ridley; we shall this day light such a candle, by God's grace, in England, as I trust shall never be put out.'

Six months later, Thomas Cranmer, Archbishop of Canterbury, was the next to be sent for trial. Losing his bottle, he signed a recantation of his Protestant beliefs, then Mary Tudor had him stuck in a pulpit to tell the world how the Catholic faith was the true faith. But halfway through the sermon he deviated from the script and was dragged out to be burnt at the same spot as Latimer and Ridley. His famous last words weren't as clever as Latimer's. As the flames rose he stuck his right hand into the fire – the hand that had signed his recantation – calling it 'that unworthy hand'. His dying words were, 'I see the heavens open and Jesus standing at the right hand of God.'

Sadly, neither God nor Jesus had a fire extinguisher handy. Nor did they have a cheque-book because the cost of supplying the faggots used to burn him were charged to the Archbishop of Canterbury's account.

The city tried, and failed, to claim the cost of the wood from the new Archbishop of Canterbury. Even the English executioners of Joan of Arc stopped short of sending the bill for the wood to the French government.

HENRY IV OF FRANCE – ASSASSINATED BY CATHOLIC FANATIC RAVAILLAC, 1610

Religion was a problem for Henry IV of France (1553–1610). Henry was another of those detested Protestants. He was King of Navarre and inherited the French throne when Henry III died. But sensing a swell of Catholic rebellion he converted to Catholicism and went to the odd church service to show his token adherence. He cynically observed, 'Paris is well worth a mass.'

It didn't fool some hard-line Catholics, and they showed their disaffection by trying to assassinate him. Twelve times.

In 1610 he was due to attend the coronation of the Queen. Like any coronation there was traffic congestion, and Henry's carriage drew to a halt. It was blocked on one side by a wine cart and on the other by a hay cart. This was just the chance the Catholic rebel François Ravaillac (1578–1610) had been waiting for.

Ravaillac was a Catholic fanatic who travelled to Paris three times to persuade Henry to convert all of the French Protestants to Catholicism. He'd had a vision telling him to do this. When he failed to get access to the King, he decided to assassinate him. And there he was at the traffic jam. He climbed onto the wheel of the King's coach and stabbed him twice.

Henry's famous last words were timeless: 'I've been stabbed.'

Without the aid of Google to diagnose his complaint, Henry IV had helpfully indicated to any doctors in the area the precise nature of his problem. The blood gushed from his mouth and that prevented any more last words.

If you're a would-be French assassin of a nervous disposition, look away now. The punishment for regicide was to have each limb attached to a wild horse and for them to set off in four directions till the victim is quartered. But before that blessed release, Ravaillac was scalded with burning sulphur, molten lead, boiling oil and resin, his flesh then being ripped by pincers. We don't have Ravaillac's last words, but they were probably not, 'Giddy-up'.

GEORGE WASHINGTON – US REVOLUTIONARY LEADER, 1799

A rebel leader like George Washington must fight tooth and nail for his cause. This was a problem for Washington as he only had one tooth by the time he was inaugurated as the first US president. His dentist soon yanked the Yankee's last one out (and kept it in a gold locket afterwards).

He had four sets of false teeth made so he could pick his teeth. There's a myth that his dentures were made of wood but that's not true. They may have been Washington's own teeth, re-mounted (except for the one the dentist kept), or fashioned from ivory or the teeth of a cow, horse or hippopotamus. Even less acceptable than ivory these days is the suggestion that some of the teeth were from enslaved people.

After his first term in office, Washington wanted to retire because of failing health but allies persuaded him to stay for four more years. He was dead within three. He developed a chill after riding round his property and fell ill with a painful throat. He told his physician: 'Doctor, I die hard, but I am not afraid to go.'*

This is just as well because he didn't have much choice. He went. His final words were to his private secretary to plan his funeral. He was afraid of being buried alive – aren't we all – so instructed the secretary to wait three days before they put him in his grave. When he was satisfied the arrangements were to his corpse's liking he (literally) croaked, "Tis well', then drew his last breath and (metaphorically) croaked.

SHAKA – ZULU LEADER, 1828

In 1787, Zulu rebel chief Shaka's mother became pregnant; she said, 'It's not a baby, it's *ishaka.*' And *ishaka* means a pain in the stomach. When the baby was born he was known as Shaka, after his mother's complaint.

He feared growing old and he believed that having children aged a man, so he murdered any of his 1,200 concubines who gave birth to a child. When Shaka's mum died he was so upset he ordered hundreds to be slaughtered.

---

* The phrase 'die hard' originated during the Battle of Albuera in 1811, in the Peninsular War. Lieutenant-Colonel William Inglis of the 57th (West Middlesex) Regiment of Foot, despite being wounded, refused to retreat and encouraged his troops to fight to the death with the rallying cry, 'Die hard, 57th, die hard!'

Shaka banned soldiers from wearing shoes so they'd toughen their feet and could run faster – up to fifty miles a day. Shaka punished any cowardly soldier with death. He also had them executed if they forgot to bring their spear to weapons training. Nor were Shaka's soldiers allowed to have girlfriends. The punishment? Death, of course.

Shaka would stand over the body of one of his victims and roar, 'Ngadla' or 'I have eaten.' Between 1815 and 1828, Shaka destroyed all the tribes in Southern Africa that were opposed to him. This chilling time became known as Mfecane or 'The Crushing'. It's estimated his rule led to the deaths of a million people. Of course, the written histories were recorded by the colonizers of the Zulu lands, so they may have been exaggerated.

By 1828, many assassination schemes had been plotted against the psychopath ruler, and they had been ruthlessly dealt with. But he trusted his half-brothers, Dingaan and Mhlangane, and met them for a chat. They turned on him and hacked him to death. As he fell, he said some great last words: 'Brothers . . . what have I done?'

Good question to be asking if you are in the middle of getting assassinated. We don't know the reply of the brothers. Probably, 'Where do you want us to start, you murderous maniac?' But the list of his crimes was too long for them to recite before he died. His body was thrown in an empty grain pot and filled with stones to stop him rising from the dead. It was then buried in an unmarked grave.

THE LAST WORD

'Give them bread and circuses and they will never revolt.'
JUVENAL (AD 55–128) – ROMAN POET

J uvenal was certainly a clever little poet and happy to share his wisdom with us lesser mortals. So, it's with some reluctance we have to say, 'Juve, lad, you are wrong if you think food and entertainment will pacify the masses. Emily Davison wasn't there for the entertainment when she was flattened by the king's horse.' Crazy Horse was aggrieved at the treatment of the US Government, and no amount of bread would have stopped him taking General Custer's life.

It's true that the French Revolution may have started with hunger and a plentiful supply of bread might well have delayed it. But the first target of the revolution was the Bastille prison – a symbol of oppressive power – and the local Greggs was not looted. Even if Marie Antoinette didn't say, 'Let them eat cake', it was the arrogance of the aristocrats that cost them their heads.

Nationalism (and the desire to determine their own fate) stirred the Māori while religion led men and women to hideous deaths by fire and bladed torture implements, rope and crushing stones. All in the name of their country or their beliefs. Sometimes an uprising can be sparked by disrespecting a golden stool.

Sometimes it is the impossible search for the beautiful but elusive ideal called 'freedom'. There is a lot of nonsense talked about freedom. That American politician Patrick Henry, who said, 'Give me liberty or give me death', has been echoed many times through history. It was rephrased by that other politician Winston Churchill (1874–1965) who said, 'You may have to fight when there is no hope of victory, because it is better to perish than to live as slaves.'

Like Juvenal, these revered men are talking nonsense. Sorry, Pat; sorry, Winnie. You can't go on rebelling against oppression if you've chosen the 'death' option. You are too dead to wave the flag of freedom as you march into the palaces of the privileged and tear the crowns off their perfumed hair.

There are assassins who try to rid the world of the worst leaders (Hitler). Sometimes the cleverest rebels are the ones who simply wait for the oppressor to die (Stalin). You can look to the past, maybe with the help of a book called *Revolting*, and weigh the causes against the consequences. What is worth rebelling for? The climate crisis? The closure of your local library?

How far would you go to progress your cause? Vote for (or stand for) the party that thinks like you? Cause a storm on social media? Sometimes the blog is mightier than the sword.

And what would you risk? Your life? (Which is pointless.) Your liberty, your health, your wealth or your happiness? Only you can decide.

When it comes to being revolting, there don't seem to be any easy answers. In the end it is down to you. You may decide your revolting actions are legally limited to the ballot box, the petition or pontificating passionately over a pint in the pub.

And back to where we started. How revolting are you?

Whatever sort of rebel you are, you can be pretty sure of one thing:

Revolt will die only with the last man.

ALBERT CAMUS (1913–60) – FRENCH WRITER

INDEX

ABOUT THE AUTHOR

Terry Deary is the author of over 350 published books, selling over 38 million copies in 45 languages.

He rose to prominence as the author of the acclaimed *Horrible Histories* series, which made him the bestselling children's non-fiction writer since records began. The series was adapted for a BAFTA-winning CBBC television series. In 2024, he published a book for adults, *A History of Britain in Ten Enemies*, which became a #1 *Sunday Times* bestseller with over 100,000 copies sold.

Terry was conferred with an honorary Doctorate of Education by Sunderland University in 2000. He lives in County Durham with his wife, Jenny, and is an avid road runner in his spare time.